Coping With Crisis

**Learning the Lessons from
Accidents in the Early Years**

Coping With Crisis

**Learning the Lessons from
Accidents in the Early Years**

Bernadina Laverty

Catherine Reay

BLOOMSBURY

LONDON · OXFORD · NEW YORK · NEW DELHI · SYDNEY

Featherstone Education

An imprint of Bloomsbury Publishing Plc

50 Bedford Square
London
WC1B 3DP
UK

1385 Broadway
New York
NY 10018
USA

www.bloomsbury.com

Bloomsbury is a registered trade mark of Bloomsbury Publishing Plc

First published 2016

British Library Cataloguing-in-Publication Data
A catalogue record for this book is available from the British Library.

ISBN:
PB 978-14729-1728-7
ePub 978-14729-1729-4
ePDF 978-14729-1730-0

Library of Congress Cataloging-in-Publication Data
A catalog record for this book is available from the Library of Congress.

10 9 8 7 6 5 4 3 2 1

Typeset by Newgen Knowledge Works (P) Ltd., Chennai, India
Printed and bound in Great Britain by CPI Group (UK) Ltd, Croydon CR0 4YY

This book is produced using paper that is made from wood grown in managed, sustainable forests. It is natural, renewable and recyclable. The logging and manufacturing processes conform to the environmental regulations of the country of origin.

To view more of our titles please visit **www.bloomsbury.com**

Disclaimer

This book is intended solely as an informative resource for early years and childcare staff. The information contained within this book has been researched and compiled from reliable sources. It is believed to be current at the time of writing. All of the accidents used as case studies within this book resulted in prosecutions under the Health and Safety at Work etc. Act 1974, unless otherwise stated. The book is intended to inform rather than advise. It provides signposts and links to useful resources. It does not negate fulfilment of statutory duties by the employer, self-employed people, employees and people in control of premises. The contents of this book may be used to assist in making informed decisions, but the user should make independent judgements appropriate to their particular setting.

The authors take no responsibility for the consequence of any error, any loss or damage suffered by the users of any information published in this book. The authors take no responsibility for inspection gradings or enforcement outcomes in settings.

For all babies and children who have lost their lives in a day care/childcare setting.
For all babies and children who have suffered life changing injuries because they attended a day care/childcare setting.
For all parents, carers and families who grieve for their children.
To take a child to a day care/childcare setting and not be able to collect that same child at home time is beyond imagining and such a tragedy.

Contents

About the authors

Bernadina Laverty is an early years consultant and previously worked as a Childcare Inspector. She has 20 years of inspection experience, covering the full range of early years provision. She has a variety of childcare experience having worked in nurseries, schools, a residential unit and with a local authority early years service. Bernadina has devised and delivered training, both in-house and as a National Vocational Qualification tutor and assessor. She holds a BA (Hons) degree in Early Childhood Studies. She has a particular interest in improving the quality of health and safety in the early years.

Catherine Reay is an environmental health professional working as a researcher for a food and health and safety consultancy. She also works as a freelance consultant. She has over 25 years of experience in health and safety and also in food safety disciplines. She has worked in both the public and private sectors. Catherine has extensive experience in auditing health and safety systems and in accident investigation. She has delivered bespoke health and safety training and devised health and safety systems across business sectors including the service and manufacturing industries. She currently designs and writes the content for online training programmes in health and safety and in food safety. She is a member of, and a registered tutor with, the Chartered Institute of Environmental Health. She has a diploma in Environmental Health and a postgraduate diploma in Management Studies. She is committed to providing practical health and safety guidance to this sector.

Previously published by the authors:
   Health and Safety in Early Years and Childcare: Contextualising health and safety legislation within the Early Years Foundation Stage (National Children's Bureau (NCB), London, 2014)

Acknowledgements

In analysing the cases outlined in this book, our purpose is not to apportion blame, but to try and highlight common areas of weak practice that can be challenging and in turn make children vulnerable. Indeed, the very nature of accidents means that they can happen at any time, in any setting, regardless of Ofsted inspection judgements.

We would like to acknowledge and thank all providers who strive every day to meet the various requirements and legislation in order to keep children safe and happy and to help them to reach their full potential. We would also like to thank all the families, where accidents have left an indelible mark on their lives.

In particular, we would both like to thank:

Helen Diamond at Bloomsbury for her patience, encouragement and suggestions throughout the writing and publication process. Her support has been invaluable.

Our friends and families, who have supported and encouraged us throughout the writing process, particularly:

Pete, Al, Sinead and Catherine for supporting and encouraging us along the way.

Fionnuala Lenehan and Diane Gilbert for their proofreading and inspirational critiques.

The Sisters of Charity of St. Paul the Apostle, Selly Park, whose kindness, encouragement and support has been invaluable.

Linda, who has provided support and encouragement from the very start of this process in 2004.

Nick Balmforth MBE, who has continued to pioneer for children's safety, both in play and in their learning environments. He is a tireless campaigner on children's safety. It is an honour that he has read and endorsed our book.

The families of all children who have died or suffered life changing injuries in day care settings.

Introduction

Who is the book for?

This book is intended for all staff working with children in settings registered on the Early Years Register (EYR) and the Childcare Register (CCR/VCR). Anyone with a general interest in child safety and accident prevention will also find this book a helpful resource. We hope that it will become invaluable for senior staff and managers who are managing health and safety in settings and as a discussion tool for team meetings and for staff development.

What is the book about?

This book focuses on real accidents and situations and looks at what went wrong in order to try and prevent future occurrences. Most of the accidents highlighted, occurred prior to the introduction of the EYR and CCR. In order to contextualise each accident relevant to practice today, we have linked the accidents under the Statutory Framework for the Early Years Foundation Stage (EYFS) 2014, the CCR/VCR 2014 and the Health and Safety at Work etc. Act 1974. The Childcare Act 2006 and associated regulations set out the requirements with which providers must comply and against which their provision is regulated. This includes the Statutory Framework for the EYFS. Providers may be registered on the Early Years Register (EYR) and/or the Childcare Register, which has two parts: the compulsory part (CCR) and the voluntary part (VCR).

The main themes of the book are:

- **Actions have consequences:** thinking about human error and analysing the circumstances around case studies.
- **Classification:** looking at the types of accidents, injuries and incidents that occur.
- **Enforcement:** looking at the legal process from two legislative perspectives: the EYFS and the Health and Safety at Work etc. Act 1974.
- **Learning the lessons for the future:** focusing on key areas in order to nurture an ongoing safety conscious culture based on the principles of 'Plan, Do, Check and Act'.

How the book can be used

This book is designed to be a resource that can be used to promote discussions and reflection on practice. The main objectives are to:

- **Highlight** the importance of prioritising children's safety.
- **Improve** practitioners' skills, knowledge and practice of keeping children safe and promoting their welfare.
- **Reiterate** the importance of personal responsibility in ensuring children can play and learn safely by looking at the outcomes of tragedies and incidents.

In each chapter we have included wherever possible, an accident overview, reporting mechanisms and a definition of the accident type. Where possible, we have also included relevant statistics. Whilst the Health and Safety Executive collates and provides an analysis of reportable injuries, diseases and incidents, the sector definitions are broad. However, in the childcare sector, there are no government departments or agencies collating records of deaths, serious injuries and accidents following notifications from providers. Therefore our research is based on press information and anecdotal evidence.

We have used case studies to examine the circumstances around each accident in more detail, making links with the The Statutory Framework for the EYFS and CCR/VCR. Each case study is then examined from a Health and Safety point of view. The legislation breached is identified in each case, where legal proceedings have been taken. The points for reflection and learning at the end of each case study or chapter would make a useful focus for a team meeting or to aid staff development in general.

There are a number of prompts that are highlighted throughout the book. These are:

Reflection: Encourage the reader to take time to: *Stop, Think, Action.*

Key points: Highlight particular important points.

Back to the team: Discussion points for providers, managers and their staff to consider and discuss.

For the agenda: Contains topics to be considered as agenda items throughout the chapters based on the topic covered.

This simple checklist is based on the Health and Safety Executive's model of the four simple steps to manage health, safety and welfare at work as an integral part of any business (www.hse.gov.uk).

To conclude each chapter, we have included safety campaigns or references to where you might find more information. Where appropriate, we have included a 'We also remember' section to acknowledge children who have suffered a life changing injury or, even more tragically, died.

1 Accidents: an overview

Chapter overview

'There's no tragedy in life like the death of a child. Things never get back to the way they were.' (Dwight D. Eisenhower, American President)

Accidents are a part of everyday life but fatalities and serious accidents have life-changing consequences for the victim, their family, the provider, the setting, the staff and the wider community. According to The Royal Society for the Prevention of Accidents (RoSPA), 'children under the age of five are most likely to be injured following a home accident. These age groups also have a greater likelihood of sustaining severe injuries with major or long term consequences' (RoSPA Position Statements, September 2014, p16). Unfortunately, children who attend day care settings are not exempt from accidents and injuries either, despite registered settings being regulated by Ofsted.

We have looked at childcare cases dating back to the millennium, and our research has shown that at least one child has died or sustained a life-changing injury or required emergency medical treatment/hospitalisation every year since 2000, while attending a day care setting. With no centralised early years/childcare data to refer to, our research has focused on both Health and Safety Executive (HSE) prosecution data and press articles. Not all cases have resulted in prosecutions and some are still going through the judicial process. For the purposes of this book we have only selected cases where there have been successful prosecutions. According to our research, the deaths to date of children, while being cared for by childminders, have been as a result of 'shaking' and are therefore not covered in this book, as these cases were deemed to be non-accidental.

Definition of an accident

An accident is a sequence of unplanned events that results in an injury or ill health. The consequences may range from a fatality, to life changing, serious or minor injuries and/or occupational illnesses. A 'near miss' is an incident where no harm occurs, but there is a potential for injury or ill health. Most accidents are preventable where sensible and proportionate risk management techniques are put into place and precautions are understood and are followed.

Accident sequence

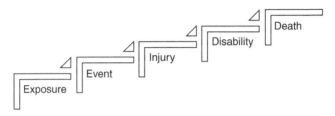

(Source: *Injury Surveillance Guidelines, World Health Organisation, 2001*)

Background research and statistics

In the UK, 60 children per year die as a result of an accident/incident in the home, with 450,000 having to attend accident and emergency (A&E) departments (Public Health England report, 'Reducing unintentional injuries in and around the home among children under five years', 2014, p4). Following the tragic deaths of three children in childcare settings in 2012, *Nursery World* magazine conducted an investigation. It revealed that there is no collation of data by Ofsted or any central government departments regarding information from deaths, accidents or serious incidents in childcare and early years settings following notifications by providers (Gaunt, C., *Nursery World*, 14 January 2013). This is despite providers being required to notify Ofsted under the Statutory Framework for the Early Years Foundation Stage (EYFS), 2014. Point 3.51 of the EYFS framework states that all registered providers must notify Ofsted of any deaths, serious accidents, incidents, illnesses and action taken. The requirement also states, 'Notification must be made as soon as is reasonably practicable, but in any event within 14 days of the incident occurring. A registered provider, who, without reasonable excuse, fails to comply with this requirement, commits an offence.' (Statutory Framework for the EYFS, 2014, p26).

The *Nursery World* article in 2013 also included comments from the Child Accident Prevention Trust (CAPT), saying it was concerned that Ofsted did not keep data on accidents in day care settings. Katrina Phillips, Chief Executive of CAPT, added, 'It's concerning that Ofsted doesn't collate data on serious accidents in early years settings and a real missed opportunity. By collating, analysing and feeding back data, Ofsted could alert settings to common problems and emerging issues. And this would provide a sound basis for local work designed to keep children safe from serious harm.' As part of our research for this book, we submitted a Freedom of Information request (FoI) to Ofsted, requesting specific information about accident, incident and diseases notifications to Ofsted dating back to 2000. Our request was refused in its original form, the response stating that the information is held in such a way that would require significant manual intervention and be prohibitive to the cost of the request. The response outlined the notification process and confirmed that all notifications received are subject to a risk assessment to ascertain if further investigation is required as outlined in the Compliance Handbook.

We were disappointed to read in the FoI response, that notifications are not passed on to other government departments, local authorities or agencies unless there is a safeguarding concern or the provider has not made the appropriate referrals. We feel this is a wasted opportunity in terms of future accident analysis and prevention and would propose that Ofsted or a central government department operate a similar system to that of the HSE. Statistics on 'reportable specified injuries', including fatalities that relate to the workplace and work activities, are collated and produced annually by the HSE. These are 'specified injuries' and conditions that require notification under the Reporting of Injuries, Diseases and Dangerous Occurrences Regulations 2013 (RIDDOR). However, the categories of industry used in these statistics are broad. The information only relates to fatalities and serious injuries that require notification under the regulations and these fall into the allocated sector category that encompasses a broad range of business activities.

By collating accident data, the HSE has been able to target enforcement action, including advice and inspection, ensuring that its inspectors and those of the local authority target resources where they are required. This has resulted in focused campaigns with the aim of maximising resources and improving health and safety outcomes. There are various organisations, including CAPT and RoSPA, which analyse data relating to accidents in the home and issue guidance accordingly. The location tends to be a key factor in how children die as a result of accidents. According to RoSPA, fire tends to be the biggest killer of children in the home.

Key point ⚯

Our research has shown that the main cause of children sustaining fatal accidents in nurseries, day care settings or playgroups is due to asphyxiation.

Accidents resulting in children's deaths

The graph on the next page gives an overview of the types of accidents resulting in deaths of children in day care settings since the millennium. It is clear that asphyxiation, be it choking or strangulation, is the biggest killer of babies and children, with children aged two years and under being the most vulnerable.

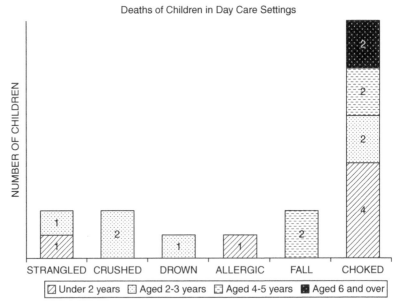
Accidents resulting in life changing injuries, emergency medical treatment and/or hospitalisation

The graph below gives an overview of the various types of accidents sustained by children while in day care settings since the millennium. It is clear that finger trapping still poses a huge risk to children, with two incidents in 2014. This is very disappointing as this type of accident is so easily preventable and is most certainly life changing as children have had whole fingers amputated, or have lost fingertips or parts of their fingers. There are many safety devices on the market that are designed to prevent entrapment. For more information of finger trap accidents, please refer to Chapter 6: Finger trapping.

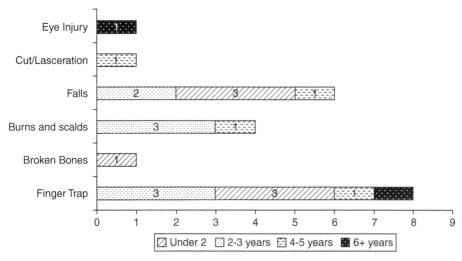

Injuries to Children in Day Care Settings

(Source: *Research collated from various press articles, 2000–15*)

For more information on any of the above data, see 'Injuries to children in day care' in the Useful links section at the end of the book.

Accident investigation

The purpose of any accident investigation is to establish the facts. This is done by an objective and analytical examination of the evidence to determine the **immediate, root** and **underlying causes** and other contributing factors that led to the event.

The immediate cause of an accident is the obvious cause of the accident for example an employee slips over and hurts themselves or a guard is missing from a piece of equipment and the user cuts their finger on the exposed cutting blade. There may be more than one immediate cause per event.

Root causes are also usually less obvious than immediate causes and must be established as part of the investigation. They are the starting point from where the failures that led to the other causes commenced. They often relate to management issues, a lack of planning and organisational failures. If root causes are not identified and dealt with, then they will occur again and cause other failures to happen in the future.

Underlying causes are less obvious and again are often identified during the process of the investigation. They can relate to failure to maintain procedures, requirements and/or failure to risk assess adequately.

The following case study illustrates this.

Case study: Salford City Council

In a prosecution case taken by the HSE, Salford City Council was fined £20,000 in Crown Court and ordered to pay costs of £3,632 following an accident at Springwood Special Educational Needs Primary School, Barton Road in Swinton. The prosecution was taken after an accident where a six-year-old pupil with autism and learning difficulties lost the tips of three fingers when his left hand became trapped in a school gate.

The risk of children trapping their hands in the outside gates had been highlighted to the council previously in a report in 2004. At the time of the accident there was a risk assessment in place. This advised staff to control the risk of entrapment by vigilance and supervision. Staff had opened the gate to allow ten children into the playground and the pupil's hand became trapped at some point while the children walked through.

Guards were only fitted to these and other gates at the school after this accident happened.

After the hearing, HSE Inspector Emily Osborne said: 'Teachers did their best to supervise children through the gates and follow the risk assessment to avoid fingers being trapped, but no action was taken by the council to prevent this from happening' (http://press.hse.gov.uk/2014/salford-council-prosecuted-after-child-loses-fingertips-in-school-gate/?ebul=hsegen&cr=10/14-apr-14).

Immediate, root and underlying causes of this accident

What allowed this accident to happen?

In this case the council failed to meet its duty to ensure the health and safety of persons not at work but affected by the work activity in 'so far as is reasonably practicable'. The cost of fitting the guard to the gate was low and the risk of injury was well known, the consequences were severe and the chance of injury was high.

While vigilance and supervision may have been an interim measure when the risk was first highlighted and while the guards were sourced and fitted, it was not a long-term solution to remove or reduce the risk. Measures taken to deal with risks need to be practical and effective. The fitting of guards to the gates was a reasonable action to take, proportionate to the risk involved.

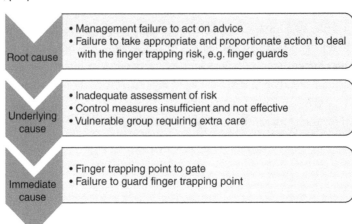

Root cause
- Management failure to act on advice
- Failure to take appropriate and proportionate action to deal with the finger trapping risk, e.g. finger guards

Underlying cause
- Inadequate assessment of risk
- Control measures insufficient and not effective
- Vulnerable group requiring extra care

Immediate cause
- Finger trapping point to gate
- Failure to guard finger trapping point

Coroners' prevention of future deaths reports

Historically, Coroners have escalated their concerns and called for change as a result of children dying. These were previously known as 'Coroners' Rule 43 Reports'. They were issued 'when the evidence at an inquest gives rise to a concern that the circumstances of this particular death create a risk of other deaths occurring in the future' (Guidance on attending an inquest, Ofsted, April 2011, No. 110012). The Chief Coroner assumed responsibility in July 2013 and Rule 43 Reports are now known as 'Prevention of Future Deaths Reports'.

Following an inquest, Coroners may send a report of the circumstances of a death to an organisation or interested party, if the Coroner is concerned that there is evidence to suggest that circumstances creating a risk of future deaths exist. The organisation must then respond within 56 days, setting out details of action they are taking, or an explanation of why none is proposed. These reports and their responses are published by the Ministry of Justice twice a year. Two cases were highlighted in Coroners' Rule 43 Reports between 1 October 2010 and 31 March 2011 that related to early years settings. The first was in response to the death of Rhiya Malin in 2007, where a request was sent to Casterbridge Nurseries 'to consider its purchasing policy for toys and playground equipment and its policy of staff using mobile phones while on duty' (www.nurseryworld.co.uk).

The second case was Adam Milner, aged two, who died in 2009 when he choked on a sausage at mealtime. The sausage had been cut up for him, but unfortunately this helped to form a plug in his throat, causing him to choke to death. Ofsted responded that it would consider a review of first aid training provided to nursery nurses and information provided to nurseries on food preparation (www.gov.uk).

The HSE has guidance on Coroners' inquests, which can be found here: http://www.hse.gov.uk/enforce/enforcementguide/wrdeaths/chronology.htm.

Human factors

Managing human failings is an essential part of accident prevention and should also be considered during any accident/incident investigation. Accidents are caused by unsafe actions, unsafe conditions or a combination of both. To understand human failings, you must also consider human factors at work.

The HSE defines human factors as:

- what people are being asked to do (the job and its requirements)
- who is doing it (the individual and their competence)
- where the job is taking place (organisation and its attributes: culture, management, communications, resources and leadership).

All three of these factors are influenced in turn by the wider social factors at both a local and national level.

Human failings that lead to unsafe acts can be divided into two distinct categories:

- errors/mistakes
- violations.

The first of these (errors/mistakes) refers to unintentional acts and the latter (violations) is intentional.

Errors include slips and lapses such as forgetting to do something. Slips and lapses may be due to a lack of attention or lapse in concentration. It is difficult to address these issues through training and they really need to be addressed by designing the job to improve levels of job satisfaction and mental well-being and by encouraging worker involvement and participation.

Mistakes are also errors but they are errors of judgement or decision-making. The intended action is wrong but it is believed to be right at the time. This type of error can be addressed through having robust safety procedures and the training of staff by a competent person. Factors that influence errors include poor design, distraction, time, pressure, competence, workload, morale and communication systems.

Violations differ because they are intentional actions. They may be made for seemingly good reasons such as getting the job done. However, they may involve taking short cuts, ignoring safety procedures, following accepted custom and practice and staff adopting poor practice from each other. Violations also include deliberate acts of sabotage. An important way of managing violations is to provide a system to detect them, for example through regular health and safety audits and inspections. In this way relevant, clear, concise and sensible proportionate rules are more likely to be followed, particularly where staff can understand the reason behind the rule. Also involving staff in health and safety rule-making and risk assessments helps to promote ownership and acceptance.

Think about injury surveillance

Definition of injury surveillance from the World Health Organisation (WHO):
'the ongoing and systematic collection, analysis, interpretation and dissemination of health information. It involves the keeping of records on individual cases, assembling information from those records, analysing and interpreting this information, and reporting it to others' (World Health Organisation, Injury Surveillance Guidelines, 2004: www.who.int).

> **Reflection**
>
> STOP
>
> - Consider the human factors.
>
> THINK
>
> - Is everyone meeting the legal requirements in your setting?
> - Is everyone professionally alert?
> - Are staff alert to children's curiosity and sense of adventure?
>
> ACTION
>
> - Evaluate where you are now. Where do you want to be?
> - How will you get there?

Keeping up-to-date

Providers working with children have experienced huge changes to guidance and legislation relating to early years and childcare in the last 25 years and particularly since the millennium. Changes have affected all aspects of caring for children including:

- Legislative changes relating to data and freedom of information.
- Safeguarding children procedures.
- Recruitment procedures for staff.
- Childcare standards.

- How children are educated and their learning and development is assessed.
- How early years is funded.
- Training qualifications for staff.

Against this backdrop of change it is understandable for practitioners to feel overwhelmed and consequently for practice to result in errors, mistakes or violations, even with the best of intentions. The table at the end of the book gives a full overview of changes.

Key point ⚬—O

- Remember, keeping up-to-date applies to new products/resources/equipment because hazards change as new products emerge.

Reflection

(STOP)

- Think about how changes are implemented in your setting.

 THINK

- Are individuals resistant to change?
- Are individuals supported in adopting changes through training, discussions, supervision?

 ACTION

- Include change management as part of supervision discussions and team meetings.
- Ascertain parents' views on how changes are implemented.

A personal value

Health and safety is about people, training and behaviour and needs to be adopted as a **personal value**. What does this look like in your setting?

- Working safely
- Being responsible and accountable for actions
- Caring for others' safety
- Reporting all accidents and near misses

- Speaking up if you see poor practice/unsafe behaviour
- Being a good role model

 ## Back to the team

Is health and safety a personal value in your team? How do you know?

 ## For the agenda

Discuss health and safety as a personal value. What does each component look like in your setting?

Accidents and child development

Babies and children have an inner drive to play and to explore their environment and, indeed, part of their developmental progress is about taking risks and challenging themselves. However, this all needs to happen in a safe and suitable environment, where vigilant staff can support and assist their endeavours. The table on the next page gives you an overview of developmental stages (DfE, Early Year's Outcomes, 2013) and subsequent hazards that can apply to any particular age group.

Preventing accidents does not require huge financial investment. It is about utilising common sense, knowledge, skills and a commitment to strive for professionalism. Therefore, regardless of the setting, a child's age/stage of development, the environment and an adult's behaviour can be a lethal or lifesaving combination.

> ## Key points ⚷
>
> Always remember that all children are unique, inquisitive individuals. Therefore, they can be at risk of all types of accidents at any age.
> As practitioners we need to **PERSEVERE** with safety through:
> P= Professionalism (including up-to-date first aid training)
> E= Education (staff, parents and children)
> R= Role-modelling safe behaviour
> S= Supervision and surveillance
> E= Empowerment (helping children to take responsibility for their own safety)
> V= Vigilance
> E= Evaluation and reflection
> R= Risk assessment
> E =Emergency (dialling 999, responding swiftly and appropriately)

The table below gives you an overview of developmental stages (Early Year's Outcomes, 2013 DfE) and subsequent hazards that can apply to any particular age group.

Age	Stage of development	Accident risks and prevention
0–11 months	Rolling, wriggling, holding objects, sucks, puts everything in the mouth	**Falls** (supervision is crucial) • Don't leave babies on a raised surface when changing nappies. • Use stair gates to prevent access to hazardous places, such as stairs, kitchen, cellars etc.
8–20 months	Crawling, rolling, sitting, beginning to stand, walking sideways around furniture, taking first steps. Can pick up objects using pincer grip. Keen to explore environment, will try to reach, climb	**Choking hazards** (particularly from food, small objects such as buttons, coins, toys and button batteries and nappy sacks) • Keep small objects and dangerous substances out of reach. • Prepare food such as sausages, carrots, apples etc. carefully to ensure they do not pose choking risks to children. Supervision at mealtimes is crucial. • Educate practitioners and parents about the dangers of items such as batteries that can be found in mobile phones, electronic toys.
16–26 months	More confident movements, fascinated by stairs	
22–36 months	More adventurous now. Walking, running, climbing, kicking, walks up and down stairs holding rails, good hand control and likes to use jugs to pour	
30–50 months	Moving and climbing confidently, sometimes overconfident. Running with speed, balancing on one foot. More confident hand control to use tools and equipment such as scissors. Likes to be helpful and can understand instructions although may not realise dangers	**Strangulation** • Ensure trailing cables, flexes, cords, ribbons are secure. • Avoid adding ropes or drawstring bags to equipment that is accessible by children. • Educate practitioners and parents about the dangers of blind cords and anything children can become entrapped in.
40–60+ months	Experiments with movements, jumping, runs with speed, good balance and coordination, using tools with increased control. Independent and adventurous	**Falls** • Be aware of the location of furniture in relation to windows. Could children climb up and fall out of a window? **Finger trapping** • Be aware of the finger trap hazards in your setting. Fit door guards wherever possible. **Burns and scalding** • Ensure hot drinks and substances such as gravy or custard are out of reach at mealtimes. **Over confidence** • Reward good safety behaviour, be alert to the pressure children may feel from their peer group to be daring or take risks. Empower children through safety education and encourage them to take responsibility for their own safety.

Back to the team

- Think about accidents, risks and prevention with your key group of children.
- Do you discuss these risks as part of your supervision sessions?

Safety campaigns

Parents who have had children die or sustain life-changing injuries in day care settings have also been influential in instigating change. An inspirational example of this is the first aid campaign led by Joanne and Dan Thompson, whose daughter Millie choked to death in 2012. As a result of their tireless campaigning, from September 2016 all newly qualified staff with a Childcare level 2 and 3 qualification will need to have completed emergency paediatric first aid or be in possession of a full paediatric first aid certificate. They have also introduced a special certificate, known as 'Millie's Mark', to be awarded to settings which achieve gold standard. This bravery and dedication in the face of such tragic adversity is an inspirational example of drive, motivation and commitment to us all. For more information on this change, see https://www.gov.uk/government/news/first-aid-training-to-be-made-compulsory-for-new-nursery-recruits.

Reflection

- Discuss the following questions.

- Do the learning and development requirements take priority in your setting?
- Are you considering child activities and near misses?
- Are you thinking about the food being served, including fruit and vegetables? How do you rate choking hazards at mealtimes in your setting?
- Are all your staff confident and competent in dealing with accidents and injuries?
- Are staff trained first aiders?
- How are changes to guidance/legislation implemented in your setting?

- Rate your current practice in relation to the above questions and justify your answers.
- Devise an action plan to address any areas of concern.

Back to the team

- In the quest for an outstanding judgement, is children's safety being compromised?
- Discuss in particular 'free-flow' play areas. In trying to introduce innovative play experiences for children, is children's safety being compromised?
- Are risk assessments completed/updated?

2 Reporting mechanisms

Chapter overview

The EYFS Statutory Framework 2014 clearly outlines the provider's duty to notify any serious accidents, incidents of food poisoning, serious illnesses or injuries sustained by children. Notifications must be made within 14 days of an incident occurring. Failure to make the relevant notifications, without a reasonable excuse, is an offence. The Ofsted notification form can be found here: www.ofsted.gov.uk.

Providers need to be aware that making notification to other agencies such as their Health and Safety Enforcing Authority does not negate their responsibility to notify Ofsted. Each regulating body must be notified separately.

Recording accidents for health and safety purposes

The Social Security (Claims and Payments) Regulations, 1979 state that if you are an employer and you employ more than ten people you are required to keep an accident book. This is used for recording accidents, injuries and incidents. You can keep the accident record electronically as long as you can retrieve this information. The other law relating to accident reporting that also requires the 'responsible person' to keep records of certain types of accidents, incidents and work related diseases is known as RIDDOR 2013. RIDDOR stands for the Reporting of Injuries, Diseases and Dangerous Occurrences Regulations. The regulations detail the types of injuries, incidents and occupational illnesses that have to be notified to the enforcing authority by a business. The enforcing authority is the body that enforces health and safety laws in that particular type of business. This will be either the local Environmental Health Department within the local authority or the HSE. RIDDOR 2013 also applies to self-employed people at work. Providers need to have a robust system in place for recording accidents, 'near misses', incidents and cases of occupational illnesses.

What should you record in an accident book/accident form?

RIDDOR 2013 (Regulation 12 and Schedule 1, Parts 1 and 2) states what type of injuries, incidents and illnesses you need to keep a record of and what information should be recorded. These include work related deaths, reportable injuries, 'over three day' injuries, dangerous occurrences and reportable occupational illnesses. The information must be kept for three years from the date when the record was made.

Schedule 1 Part 2 tells you what information to record:

- Date and time of the accident or incident
- Details about the injured employee:
  - full name
  - occupation
  - nature of injury
- Details of the injured person (if accident involves a person not at work):
  - full name
  - status (for example, 'customer', 'visitor' or 'child')
  - nature of injury
- Place where the accident or incident happened
- A brief description of the circumstances in which the accident or incident happened
- Date when the accident or incident was notified to the enforcing authority
- How the notification was made to the enforcing authority

Key points ⚊O

- It is also a good idea to make a note of the details of any witnesses to the accident and to detail any first aid treatment given.
- Data protection requires that all personal information must be kept safe.

Reportable accidents

RIDDOR 2013 Regulation 3: Who is the 'responsible person?'

The 'responsible person' has a duty to notify certain types of accident, incident or occupational illness that occur at work, to the enforcing authority. The definition of the responsible person can change depending on circumstances. In most cases, and certainly when notifying an accident to an employee at work, the responsible person is their employer. Certain accidents and injuries involving 'non-workers' are also reportable. This category of person would include the children in your care and any visitors. In this case, the person in control of the premises and the business activity is the responsible person. If the injured person is a self-employed worker then the responsible person can change, depending where the accident took place.

If an accident takes places involving a self-employed person at work in premises where the self-employed person is not on their own business premises, then the accident needs to be notified by the person in control of the premises where the work activity took place. This situation would apply to a contractor working at your premises.

Reportable accidents to 'workers'

RIDDOR requires that the responsible person must notify the following types of injury to their employees that arise from an accident at work.

RIDDOR 2013 Regulation 6: Work-related fatalities

- All deaths arising out of, or in connection with, work whether or not that person died at the workplace.
- If the person is an employee, even if the death occurs up to a year after the accident has taken place, it must still be notified. This is in addition to any previous notification made at the time that the accident took place.

RIDDOR 2013 Regulation 4 (1): Non-fatal injuries to workers

These are called 'specified injuries' in the guidance to the regulations. They are:

- any bone fracture diagnosed by a registered medical practitioner, other than to a finger, thumb or toe
- amputation of an arm, hand, finger, thumb, leg, foot or toe
- any injury diagnosed by a registered medical practitioner as being likely to cause permanent blinding or reduction in sight in one or both eyes
- any crush injury to the head or torso causing damage to the brain or internal organs in the chest or abdomen
- any burn injury (including scalding) which covers more than 10% of the whole body's total surface area; or
- causes significant damage to the eyes, respiratory system or other vital organs
- any degree of scalding requiring hospital treatment
- loss of consciousness caused by head injury or asphyxia
- any other injury arising from working in an enclosed space which
  - leads to hypothermia or heat-induced illness; or
  - requires resuscitation or admittance to hospital for more than 24 hours.

Notifying a death or a non-fatal injury to workers

The notification procedure is detailed in Schedule 1 of RIDDOR 2013 and requires the responsible person to make the notification to the enforcing authority by the 'quickest practicable means'. This means a telephone call to the Incident Contact Centre on 0345 300 9923 (opening hours Monday to Friday 8.30 am to 5 pm). The telephone notification must be followed up by the completion and submission of an online notification form, which must be received within ten days of the accident occurring. This form is called 'Report of an Injury'.

You will receive a copy of this form once you have submitted it online. It is your record of the reportable accident and notification. You can find advice on the HSE website at www. hse.gov.uk. There is also information about how to make notifications outside of working hours.

Non-reportable 'over three day' injuries

Since 6 April 2012, 'over three days' injuries to persons at work where they are incapacitated for over three consecutive days, as a result of an accident at work, are no longer reportable injuries. You are still required to keep a record of this type of accident but you are not required to notify it. You need to record it in your accident book and ensure you have the following details as required in Schedule 1 Part 2 of RIDDOR 2013:

- date and time of the accident
- particulars of the injured person: full name, occupation and nature of injury
- place where the accident happened
- a brief description of the circumstances in which the accident happened.

Reportable 'over seven day' injuries

RIDDOR 2013 Regulation 4 (2) states there is a requirement to notify an injury that results in the incapacity of a person at work for more than seven consecutive days.

Guidance states that when calculating the consecutive incapacity days you need to consider non-work days, such as days off shift, weekends, holidays or when the injured person was not due to work anyway. Ask the injured person to confirm whether, if they had to work, they would have been able to do so. If they were not capable of working or carrying out their normal duties on these non-work days, you need to include these days when calculating the 'over seven day period' and the 'over three day period'. You do not include the day of the accident when calculating the consecutive days.

Guidance also states that if an employee is unable to carry out their full range of duties for more than seven consecutive days as a result of an accident at work, then it is still a reportable injury. The report needs to be made within 15 days of the accident. In the event of the incapacity developing later and resulting in a more than seven consecutive days' absence from work, then the report must be made within 15 days of that absence.

How to notify an 'over seven day' injury

The responsible person must complete and submit the online notification form. This must be received within 15 days of the accident occurring. This form is called 'Report of an Injury'. You will receive a copy of this form once you have submitted it online. It is your record of the reportable accident and notification. You can find advice at www.hse.gov.uk.

Incidents of non-consensual violence to employees

RIDDOR 2013 Regulation 2(1)

The definition of an accident includes incidents of 'non-consensual' violence to people at work. Therefore, if an employee is hurt as a result of such an incident and a physical injury results, the accident may be reportable if:

- the injury is a specified injury or results in death
- the member of staff is incapacitated for more than seven consecutive days as a result of the injury.

Reportable accidents to 'non-workers'

RIDDOR 2013 Regulations 5 and 6 and Schedule 1, Parts 1 and 2

- This type of accident affects the children in your care and visitors to your premises if they are injured as a result of your business activity.

Work-related fatalities to non-workers

All deaths arising out of, or in connection with, work whether or not that person died at the workplace.

Other types of reportable injury to 'persons not at work'

These types of injury are called a 'non-fatal injuries to non-workers'. If a child in your care has an accident (that is related to your work and workplace) and is taken from the site where the accident occurred to hospital, for treatment for an injury, then this is a reportable accident and the responsible person must notify it to the enforcing authority.

It does not matter how the injured person is taken to hospital. It does not need to be by an ambulance. The accident is still reportable whether treatment was given or not, but there is no requirement to confirm what treatment has been given. Guidance states that if no injury is apparent and the accident victim is taken to hospital as a precaution only, then there is no requirement to notify in these circumstances.

The notification process for reportable accidents to non-workers is the same as for a death or a specified injury to a worker.

Dangerous occurrences

RIDDOR 2013 Regulation 7, Schedules 1 and 2
There are certain types of incidents that occur that also require notification under RIDDOR 2013. These are dangerous occurrences. They are listed in the regulations and require notification to the enforcing authority.

Occupational diseases

RIDDOR 2013 Regulation 8, Schedule 1, Part 1
RIDDOR 2013 also details certain types of illnesses that workers can develop through exposure to occupational hazards in the workplace. These are known as occupational diseases. They are listed in the regulations and require notification to the enforcing authority. Guidance about dangerous occurrences and occupational diseases and how to notify them is available on the HSE website at http://www.hse.gov.uk/riddor/report.htm.

Offences

It is an offence under the Health and Safety at Work Etc. Act 1974 to fail to comply with health and safety regulations. Therefore, if you fail to notify a reportable accident, incident or occupational disease as required under RIDDOR 2013 you are committing an offence. Late reporting is also an offence; you will read a case study later where this occurred.

Are you up to date with RIDDOR?

The 2013 regulations aim to simplify the requirements placed on businesses. There have been changes to the list of specified injuries, incidents and diseases that you are required to notify. Previous guidance on RIDDOR 1995 (as amended) has been replaced to reflect these changes. The HSE has also produced a simple guide called 'Reporting accidents and incidents at work. A brief guide to the Reporting of Injuries, Diseases and Dangerous Occurrences Regulations 2013' (RIDDOR). You can obtain this and other up-to-date information on RIDDOR by visiting the HSE website at www.hse.gov.uk.[1]

EYFS notification links

EYFS Link
* 3.50 Requirements for accident recording
* 3.54 Requirements for complying with Health and Safety legislation
* (Department for Education. Statutory Framework for the Early Year Foundation Stage 2014. p26).

CCR Link
* CR 8 Records to be kept
* CR 13 Matters affecting the welfare of children
* (Ofsted. 2014 Requirements for the Childcare Register: childcare providers on nondomestic or domestic premises. No. 080143)

Outbreaks of an infectious disease and/or gastroenteritis

An outbreak is defined as 'two or more linked cases of the same disease or when the observed number of cases unaccountably exceeds the expected number' (http://food.gov.uk).

As you will see from our case study in Chapter 10, outbreaks of food poisoning and gastroenteritis can spread rapidly in a setting if strict exclusion, meticulous personal hygiene and environmental controls are not in place. Providers need to be ready and prepared to deal with outbreaks should they arise. This means having a plan to respond quickly to reduce the risk of the infection spreading. The plan should include notifying and liaising with Environmental Health and your regional Public Health Unit. If there is an outbreak at a setting then this is likely to trigger an enforcement visit. The purpose of this visit will be to determine whether the outbreak is a viral outbreak such as 'norovirus' or an outbreak of food poisoning or a foodborne illness. The Enforcement Officer is likely to complete a food safety inspection to check this, as well as gathering information about the cases and assessing your controls.

Where to go for help and guidance

Public Health England has produced guidance on infection control entitled 'Guidance on infection control in schools and other child care settings'. This can be downloaded from the Government website at https://www.gov.uk.

The Health Protection Agency (HPA) has been replaced by Public Health England, Public Health Scotland, Public Health Wales and the Public Health Agency in Northern Ireland. Your local Environmental Health Department is also a useful source of help and information. Guidance on dealing with cases of infectious diseases and outbreaks is available on many local authority websites. Environmental Health Practitioners/Officers and Food Safety Officers will also give you advice.

Reflection

- Do staff know what accidents and incidents are reportable under RIDDOR 2013?

- Do you have a system for accident/incident/near miss reporting?

- How do you know that this system is working? When did you last check?

 For the agenda

- How do we record and report accidents and incidents?
- How many accidents, incidents and near misses have taken place since the last meeting?

EYFS notification links

In addition to the requirements regarding notifications under RIDDOR 2013, the Statutory Framework for the EYFS also requires providers to notify Ofsted.

EYFS Link

- 3.49 Requirements for reporting food poisoning

(Department for Education. Statutory Framework for the Early Year Foundation Stage 2014. p26).

CCR Link

- CR 13 Matters affecting the welfare of children

(Ofsted. 2014 Requirements for the Childcare Register: childcare providers on non domestic or domestic premises. No. 080143)

Reflection

- Consider the documentation in your setting and your notification procedures. Are all staff aware of their individual responsibilities?

- Are line management responsibilities explicit to all staff?
- Are notifications clear, traceable and followed up?
- Do your induction procedures include the notifications process?

- Evaluate your documentation and notification procedures and prioritise areas of concerns to be addressed.

3 Asphyxiation

Chapter overview

While most accidents are preventable, accidents involving asphyxiation are often fatal and are the biggest cause of death to children under five (HPA, 'Reducing unintentional injuries in and around the home among children under five years', 2014, p8). Babies and young children are particularly susceptible to these types of accidents as their inquisitiveness means they are prone to putting things in their mouths and around their necks. Food in particular has posed a huge choking risk to babies and young children due to the size, shape and texture of foods such as fruit, sausages and mashed potato. Asphyxiation can be due to:

- suffocation
- choking
- strangulation.

In order to analyse and reflect on fatalities due to asphyxiation, we have chosen just four cases where children have died, to explore in more depth. We have added links at the end of this chapter for all of the other children that have died so tragically due to asphyxiation.

Definition of asphyxiation

Asphyxiation is 'the state or process of being deprived of oxygen, which can result in unconsciousness or death or suffocation' (Oxford English Dictionary).

Statistics

According to CAPT, asphyxiation related accidents cause 28 children under five to die each year. Every day 50 children are hospitalised with a choking related accident.

As part of our research for this book, we compiled the table opposite to show the number of children who have died in day care settings due to asphyxiation since 2000, with choking clearly being the biggest risk to young children.

Fatalities due to Asphyxiation
in Day Care since 2000

3			
2	2	2	2
	1		
UNDER 2 YEARS	2-3 YEARS	4-5 YEARS	6+ YEARS

■ Strangled ☐ Choked

(Source: *Based on various press articles, 2000–15*)

Case File 1: Cameron Lindsay, aged 7 months

Date and nature of death: March 2004, asphyxiation

Location: Sticky Fingers Nursery, Bromsgrove

Crown Court verdict: Defendant pleaded guilty.

Enforcement outcome: Nursery owner Dawn Wilson fined £12,000. £10,000 prosecution costs awarded to West Mercia Police. The nursery closed and did not re-open.

(Source: www.news.bbc.co.uk/1/hi/england/hereford/worcs/4887892.stm, article entitled 'Owner fined in nursery death case', by BBC News. Published Friday, 7 April 2006, 12:48 GMT © Copyright of BBC.

Source: www.telegraph.co.uk, article entitled 'Parents 'will be haunted forever' by face of baby who died at nursery', The Telegraph, Nick Britton. Published: 8 April 2006, 12.01 am BST © Copyright of Telegraph Media Group Limited.)

Background details

Cameron had been placed in a rock and carry cradle/rocker in the sleep room at the nursery. He had been asleep in the cradle. He was left unattended for 20 minutes. Nursery staff found him with his head wedged between the seat and the hood of the cradle. An ambulance was called and Cameron was taken to the local hospital at Redditch. He was later transferred to Birmingham Children's Hospital where he died.

Contributing factors with links to the EYFS

Supervision of children: Cameron was left unattended for 20 minutes and staff could not hear him crying as they were outside in the garden with other children. The EYFS framework 3.28 states: 'Children must usually be within sight and hearing of staff and always within sight or hearing' (DfE, Statutory Framework for the EYFS, 2014, p21). In addition, the Statutory Framework of the EYFS 3.59 states that sleeping children must be checked frequently. This did not happen in Cameron's case.

- **Lack of risk assessment:** Staff did not anticipate the potential hazard posed by the rock and carry cradle/rocker and clearly ignored the manufacturer's instructions to ensure children are always supervised when using the chair. The EYFS framework 3.64 covers risk assessment.

- **The rock and carry cradle/rocker was assembled incorrectly:** Staff did not follow the manufacturer's instructions for assembling the chair and did not check that it was safe and suitable for use by children. The EYFS framework 3.54 covers safety and suitability of equipment and highlights the need for providers to comply with other legislation, including health and safety.

- **Unqualified staff running the nursery:** The person in charge on the day the accident happened was an unqualified 19-year-old. The EYFS framework 3.23 states that managers need to have a level 3 qualification and at least two years' experience. It also identifies the need to have a capable and competent deputy who can take charge in the absence of the manager.

Contributing factors with links to the CCR/VCR

CR 1.8 Welfare of the children being cared for
CR 5.1 Suitability and safety of premises and equipment
CR 5.5 Suitability and safety of premises and equipment

Contributing factors under Health and Safety

- The rock and carry cradle was assembled incorrectly and the manufacturer's instructions were not followed.

- Cameron was left unsupervised. Staff were outside with other children and were unable to monitor him.

- There was a failure to carry out a suitable and sufficient risk assessment prior to assembling and using the equipment.

The lack of an effective health and safety management system:

- An effective system was not formalised and implemented to ensure that babies were not left unattended/unsupervised for any period of time.

- An effective system was not formalised and implemented for controlling and assessing equipment at the premises and ensuring that it was used in accordance with the manufacturer's instructions.

- An effective system was not formalised and implemented to ensure that employees were competent and were aware of their responsibilities.

Legislation breached

Failure to meet the general duty of an employer to 'persons not in their employment' under Section 3(1) of the Health and Safety at Work Etc. Act 1974:

'It shall be the duty of every employer to conduct his undertaking in such a way as to ensure, so far as is reasonably practicable, that persons not in his employment who may be affected thereby are not thereby exposed to risks to their health or safety.'[1] The offence for failing to meet this duty is detailed in Section 33(1) (a) of the Act.

Dawn Wilson and two members of staff, Nicola Hadlington and Rebecca Lamare, were initially charged with manslaughter. They were all acquitted of these charges. The Health and Safety charge was laid against Dawn Wilson only. (Source: www.news.bbc.co.uk article entitled 'Guilty plea over baby boy's death', by BBC News. Published: Friday, 3 April 2006, 11:33 GMT © Copyright of BBC).

Key point

To manage health and safety effectively you need to have identified the health and safety risks in your business.

Judge's comments

Judge David Matthews told the defendant that he was 'entirely satisfied that [she] fell short of the required standard to ensure the health and safety of that child' (Matthews, D. www.news.bbc.co.uk).

Reflection

(STOP)

- Do your risk assessments cover the real risks to staff and others in your business?

- Have you covered activities such as sleeping in your risk assessments?

- Talk to your staff and review your risk assessments to make sure you have considered all of your significant risks.

Back to the team

What are the arrangements for sleep checks? Discuss and make sure that there is no ambiguity and that all staff understand what is required in your setting.

Case File 2: Molly Cunliffe, aged 16 months

Date and nature of death: 4 November 2005, strangled

Location: Tiddlywinks Nursery, Gloucester

Crown Court verdict: Defendant pleaded guilty

Inquest verdict: Unlawful killing

Enforcement outcome: Nursery owner Rosemary Meadows was fined £35,000 and ordered to pay £20,000 prosecution costs. The nursery was sold.

(Source: www.news.bbc.co.uk article entitled 'Baby girl was "unlawfully killed"', by BBC News. Published: Thursday, 5 July 2007, 15:27 GMT © Copyright of BBC).

(Source: http://www.dailymail.co.uk/news/article-1081542/Nursery-owner-ordered-pay-55–000-showing-gross-incompetence-toddler-strangled-clothes-bag. html article entitled ' Nursery owner ordered to pay £55,000.00 for showing 'gross incompetence' after toddler strangled herself on a clothes bag' by Mail online, a Daily Mail reporter. 30 October 2008. Updated 02.02 © Copyright of Associated Newspapers Ltd, the Daily Mail, The Mail on Sunday & Metro Media Group).

Background details

Molly Cunliffe was 16 months old. She strangled herself on the cord to a drawstring clothes bag that had been left attached to the cot which she had been put in to sleep. She had been left unattended for more than 20 minutes. She had been left in the care of a 17-year-old student and an unqualified member of staff. Molly was found in a 'lifeless' condition. She was taken to hospital but died two weeks later when a decision was made to turn her life support machine off. The Prosecutor told the court that the damage was brought about by the constriction of her neck, breathing and blood flow brought about by entanglement with the cord. Molly's parents had warned staff at the nursery that Molly had developed a habit of putting things around her neck.

Contributing factors with links to the EYFS

- **Supervision of children:** Molly was left unattended for more than 20 minutes. The EYFS framework 3.28 states, 'Children must usually be within sight and hearing of staff and always within sight or hearing' (DfE, Statutory Framework for the EYFS, 2014, p21).

- **Conflict of understanding regarding sleep checks:** The policy of the nursery was to check sleeping children every ten minutes. However, staff had a conflicting understanding of how and when to conduct sleep checks, resulting in Molly being neglected. The EYFS framework 3.59 states that 'sleeping children must be checked frequently' (DfE, Statutory Framework for the EYFS, 2014, p28). Practitioners need to decide on their interpretation of 'frequently' and ensure all staff are aware of how and when to check sleeping children and how these checks are evidenced.

- **Parent's knowledge of their own child ignored by staff:** Molly's parents had warned staff that Molly was an inquisitive child who had developed a habit of putting things around her neck. Staff disregarded this vital information and left a drawstring bag tied to the cot. The EYFS framework 3.27 outlines the role of the key person and the importance of building relationships with parents. It states that 'every child's care is tailored to meet their individual needs and sleeping children must be checked frequently' (DfE, Statutory Framework for the EYFS, 2014, p21).

- **Lack of risk assessment:** Staff did not challenge the practice of leaving looped drawstring bags tied to cots. Therefore, staff did not anticipate the risk of strangulation posed by a drawstring clothes bag and no risk assessment had been carried out. The EYFS framework 3.64 covers risk assessment.

- **An unqualified staff member and a 17-year-old student were left to care for Molly:** Senior managers were having a meeting in the upstairs of the nursery on the day Molly strangled herself. While the rota may have indicated the nursery was operating within staffing ratios, the decision to deploy an unqualified member of staff and a 17-year-old student to supervise the baby room was both inappropriate and in breach of EYFS requirements relating to staff qualification, training, support and skills. The EYFS framework 3.31 outlines the requirement for staff to 'hold a full and relevant level 3 qualification and must be suitably experienced in working with children under two' (DfE, Statutory Framework for the EYFS, 2014, p22). In addition, EYFS framework 3.28 clearly states that staff must be deployed appropriately to ensure that all children are adequately supervised and their needs met. The guidance on students is covered in the EYFS framework 3.29 and outlines how staff and students aged 17 or over may be included in ratios 'if the provider is satisfied that they are competent and responsible' (DfE, Statutory Framework for the EYFS, 2014, p21).

Contributing factors with links to the CCR/VCR

CR 1.8 Welfare of the children being cared for
CR 1.12 Welfare of the children being cared for
CR 5.5 Suitability and safety of premises and equipment

Contributing factors under Health and Safety

- The presence of the drawstring bag that had been left on the cot.

- Molly had been left unsupervised.

- A misunderstanding or misinterpretation by staff of the sleep checks requirements.

- Failure to act on and communicate information provided by the parents relating to their child's behaviour.

The lack of an effective health and safety management system:

- A failure to identify and assess the strangulation risk associated with equipment/ furnishings with cords, cables and loops.

- A failure to communicate, implement and monitor an effective system to supervise and check babies and young children while sleeping.

- A failure to inform and train staff in the risk associated with cords, cables and loops and their proximity and accessibility to children.

The hazards and accidents to children arising from looped cords are well documented. RoSPA has run a lengthy safety campaign calling upon the blind industry to reduce the safety risks from looped blind cords. In February 2014, three new European Safety Standards were announced, aimed at reducing the risks to children from blind cords. In a childcare setting any loose length of material or looped material such as chain, rope or cord will present a risk of strangulation and/or entanglement if they are accessible to the babies and young children. In this situation it was usual practice to attach drawstring bags to the cots. Loose materials can also be a tripping hazard to staff and clients, depending on their location. A trailing electrical cable was also found in the nursery in an area where it posed a risk.

A suitable and sufficient risk assessment should have identified the risk to children posed by the practice of attaching drawstring bags to cots.

Legislation breached

Two charges were initially laid against the owner of the nursery. First, that the defendant had failed to ensure 'that babies and toddlers were not exposed to risks to their health and safety by failing to ensure that no cord or loop was allowed in proximity of babies and toddlers, [that] babies and toddlers were checked sufficiently regularly in their cots, and that staff were alerted to the risk associated with the cords and loops in the proximity of babies and toddlers'. Second, that she had failed to make sufficient assessment of the risk of 'entanglement and strangulation'. This charge was later withdrawn.

The first charge relates to a failure to meet the general duty of employers to 'persons not in their employment' under Section 3(1) of the Health and Safety at Work Etc. Act 1974. The offence for failing to meet this duty is detailed in Section 33(1) (a) of the Act.

Judge's comments

Crown Court Judge Mark Horton said: 'This was such an obvious risk that virtually no parent in their own home would have considered this, let alone professionals who should have been responsible.' He also said that staff had shown 'gross incompetence' in that they had failed to take notice of the warnings given by Molly's parents that she was in the habit of putting things around her neck (Horton, M: www.dailymail.co.uk).

Reflection

This is best summarised by the judge's comments (above).
Parents know their children best. Effective partnership working means parents' comments and concerns must be listened to and acted upon. This combination of failures resulted in Molly's death. If staff had heeded her parents' comments about Molly's propensity to put things around her neck, they may have anticipated the risk posed by the drawstring bag.

- Practitioners need to consider carefully how staff are deployed throughout the day. Are all children appropriately supervised and are their needs being met?

- Does everyone understand the procedures for sleep checks in your setting?
- Does everyone implement the procedures for sleep checks in your setting? How do you know?
- Think about parent/staff communication systems. How could this be improved?

- Review systems in relation to sleep checks, risk assessment and communication with parents.

Case File 3: Georgia Hollick, aged 10 months

Date and nature of death: April 2006, choked
Location: Just Learning Limited, Cambridgeshire
Inquest verdict: Accidental death
Crown Court verdict: Defendant pleaded guilty – responsible for a state of affairs where 'there was risk of death'
Enforcement outcome: £145,000 (£67,000 fine and £78,187 costs). The nursery at Cambourne in Cambridgeshire was later sold.
(Source: http://www.telegraph.co.uk/news/uknews/4969646/Nursery-company-fined-145000-for-baby-choking-death.html, article entitled 'Nursery company fined £145,000 for baby choking to death', by Telegraph News. Published: Thursday, 5 July 2007, 15:27 GMT © Copyright of Telegraph Media Group Limited).

Background details

Georgia Hollick, aged 10 months, choked to death at Just Learning Nursery in Cambridgeshire after being given an 8mm slice of fruit to eat, while sitting on the floor. The trained first aider in the setting was supervising sleeping children at the time and shouted instructions from the next room to three members of staff, whose first aid training was not up-to-date. Staff ignored Georgia's parents' request to ensure she was fed in a high chair.

Contributing factors with links to the EYFS

- **Inappropriate deployment of first aider:** The qualified first aider shouted instructions from another room where she was supervising sleeping children. The EYFS framework 3.25 outlines that 'providers should take into account the number of children, staff and layout of premises to ensure that a paediatric first aider is able to respond to emergencies quickly' (DfE, Statutory Framework for the EYFS, 2014, p21).
- **First aid training not up-to-date:** Staff who tried to save Georgia did not have up-to-date first aid training. The EYFS framework 3.25 outlines the need for a qualified first aider to be on the premises and available to children at all times.

Asphyxiation

- **Inadequate training records:** Systems in place to record and monitor staff training were ineffective as three members of staff were working in the room with expired first aid certificates. Most first aid training providers require that training is renewed every three years. Staff supervision was clearly not effective as the EYFS framework 3.21 outlines that supervision should offer opportunities for staff to discuss issues regarding professional development and outline any issues concerning children in their care. Supervision is also an ideal opportunity for management to check the status and validity of training such as first aid.

- **Failure to practise emergency procedures:** Despite the nursery's own guidelines outlining that first aid should be administered by a trained employee, Georgia was treated by three workers whose first aid certificate had expired. One of these members of staff could easily have gone to relieve the qualified first aider who was supervising sleeping children and made a difference to the outcome. Therefore, this demonstrated a failure in practising emergency procedures and an ineffective deployment of the qualified first aider.

- **Parent's knowledge of child ignored:** Staff ignored parents' requests for their child to be fed in a high chair. This demonstrated a failure by staff to acknowledge parents' wishes and ignores guidance outlined under the EYFS framework 3.27 on key persons.

- **Lack of risk assessment:** Staff clearly demonstrated a lack of understanding of the choking hazards posed by food, especially for babies and young children. The EYFS framework 3.64 covers risk assessment.

This is yet another example where parents' expert knowledge of their own child and specific request (for example, of how they preferred their child to be fed) was ignored, with tragic consequences. Policies and procedures need to be actualised in practice, in conjunction with common sense.

Contributing factors with links to the CCR/VCR

CR 1.1 Welfare of the children being cared for
CR 1.4 Welfare of the children being cared for
CR 4.3 Qualifications and training (CCR Only)

Contributing factors under Health and Safety

- The unsuitable size of food and method of feeding.
- Failure to listen to and take account of the advice and instructions given by a parent in relation to feeding.
- Failure to implement effective emergency first aid.

A lack of an effective health and safety management system:

- A failure to implement an effective system for refresher training in first aid.
- A failure to recognise and assess the risks of choking presented by food, especially for a vulnerable group such as babies and young children.

First aid

Although the Health and Safety (First Aid) Regulations 1981 do not require employers to make first aid provision for members of the public, the HSE recommends that they are considered in the first aid needs assessment and that provision is made for them. This is in circumstances where the employer is providing a service for others, for example, nurseries, schools, shops, concert halls etc. The Statutory Framework for the EYFS has separate and standalone requirements for first aid provision. First aid courses are updated, as first aid techniques can change with improvements in knowledge and information. This is why the HSE recommends that first aiders undertake annual refresher training during their three-year qualification period to ensure that their basic skills are maintained and that techniques are kept up to date.

Paediatric first aid is a specialist area and there are specific tailored courses that focus on emergency procedures to enable the first aider to assess an emergency situation safely. When selecting members of staff for first aid training, it is important to consider their personal qualities and how they will respond in an emergency. Consider:

- their reliability, disposition and communication skills.
- their ability to learn, absorb knowledge and develop a new skill.
- their ability to cope with a stressful and physically demanding emergency situation.

In addition, as part of their normal duties, they should be available and able to respond to an emergency situation quickly. Guidance on first aid requirements is available at the HSE website at www.hse.

Legislation breached

The charge related to a failure to meet the general duty of employers to 'persons not in their employment' under Section 3(1) of the Health and Safety at Work Etc. Act 1974. The offence for failing to meet this duty is detailed in Section 33(1) (a) of the Act.

Judge's comments

Judge Hawkesworth said, 'These failings had the effect of exposing children in the company's care to heightened risk for a substantial period of time' (Hawkesworth, J. www. telegraph.co.uk/news).

Reflection

- Do your staff have full, relevant and up-to-date first aid certification?

- Do you have a system in place to share parental requests for how children should be cared for?

- Do your staff know what to do in an emergency?

 Back to the team

Review and evaluate the menu in your setting. What foods pose a choking hazard?

Case File 4: Lydia Bishop, aged 3 years

Date and nature of death: 17 September 2012, strangulation
Location: York College Nursery, York
Crown Court verdict: Guilty
Enforcement outcome: £175,000 fine against York College plus £45, 000 costs (Source: http Coulson, J: 'R v York College, Leeds Crown Court 14 February 2014 Sentencing Remarks of Coulson J' https://www.judiciary.gov.uk/wp-content/uploads/JCO/Documents/Judgments/r-v-york-college.pdf Published: 14 February 2014 © Copyright of Judiciary of England and Wales).

Background details

Lydia Bishop died on her first day at nursery. She had accessed an area of the nursery garden that had been deemed out of bounds, because the area could not be seen by staff and was blocked off with an inadequate, makeshift barrier consisting of a wooden bench and plastic trolley. Lydia, unseen by staff, played on a slide in this area and became entangled on a rope that had been attached to the slide by staff. The rope was supposed to be removed at the end of every play session. Lydia caught her neck in the rope, which acted as a noose as she tried to go down the slide. Lydia lay undiscovered for 20 minutes, by which time she was dead.

Contributing factors with links to the EYFS

- **Access to the slide:** The setting installed a 'makeshift' barrier in an attempt to stop children accessing the slide. This was wholly inadequate for the purpose. Staff had previously suggested installing some fencing and a gate, but this suggestion was rejected by management. Had a fence and gate been installed, Lydia would not have had the easy access to the slide and her death may have been prevented.

- **Supervision:** Staff had identified parts of the play areas that needed specialist supervision such as the slide. It is unfortunate that they did not check this area as part of their overall supervision, especially as they were aware that the makeshift barrier was ineffective. As Lydia was new to the nursery, it should have been anticipated that she would be especially curious to investigate her new surroundings. Lydia was obviously not seen entering the restricted area and was not discovered for at least 20 minutes, by which time she was dead.

- **The rope attached to the slide:** Staff had modified the slide by adding the rope, probably to add a different dimension and challenge to children's play. While staff had considered the risks posed by the rope in their risk assessment, they failed to follow their own control measures for minimising the risk. The EYFS framework 3.54 outlines the importance of ensuring the premises and activities provided are suitable for all children. The EYFS framework 3.64 covers risk assessments and how these need to inform staff practice. It also reiterates the importance of checking the environment, the need to clearly identify who will make these checks and how risks will be removed or minimised. This omission highlights the importance of ensuring all staff are engaged in personally managing safety every day, through both documentation and practical actions, because one without the other will result in oversights and possibly tragic consequences, as happened in this case.

Key point ⚬━O

- Staff need to be wary of adapting/modifying pieces of equipment, however well intentioned the motives are. Manufacturers clearly outline how equipment is to be assembled and used in order to comply with safety checks that will have to be undertaken on such equipment.

Contributing factors with links to the CCR/VCR

CR 1.1 Welfare of the children being cared for
CR 1.4 Welfare of the children being cared for
CR 5.1 Suitability and safety of premises and equipment

Contributing factors under Health and Safety

- The slide was accessible due to an insufficient and inadequate 'barrier' being in place. Lydia was able to simply walk around the barrier.
- A length of rope 16 metres in length was attached to the slide at the time of the accident.
- The play equipment was unsupervised as it was technically out of bounds.
- The location of the slide did not afford good supervision. This was recognised as a risk. A member of staff had suggested that a fence and gate should be installed to allow access to be prohibited when adequate supervision could not be provided. The method of preventing access that was adopted was inadequate.
- The jury heard evidence that the control measure of putting the rope away after use was sometimes ignored and that the rope was left out until the end of the day.
- Failure to implement an active monitoring system through management checking and audit.
- Failure to implement and monitor a control measure that was clearly stated in the risk assessments to place ropes out of the reach of children when they were not in use.
- No one appeared to take responsibility to check that the control measure was being implemented. This included management.

Legislation breached

A charge was laid against the college for a failure to meet the general duty of employers to 'persons not in their employment' under Section 3(1) of the Health and Safety at Work Etc. Act 1974. The offence for failing to meet this duty is detailed in Section 33(1) (a) of the Act. A charge of 'gross negligence manslaughter' and an alternative health and safety charge were laid against a member of staff, Sophee Redhead but these charges were rejected by the jury. (Source: (Source: www.yorkpress.co.uk/news/10992999.York_College_guilty_over_Lydia_Bishop_death_Sophee_Redhead_cleared_UPDATED/ article entitled "York College Guilty over Lydia bishop death, Sophee Redhead cleared- UPDATED" by Megi Rychlikova. Published 07 February 2014 © Copyright of The York Press)

Judge's comments

In sentencing, Mr Justice Coulson said: 'York College made a feature of what they called "challenging" play and playing with ropes was one aspect of that. But York College was also rightly aware that the rope or ropes could cause serious harm to the children. Accordingly, as part of their health and safety regime, they produced two separate risk assessments which dealt with the use of the rope in the outside area. Those risk assessments expressly identified that the rope posed to the children the risk of strangulation. There were two particular control measures identified to deal with that risk: putting the ropes out of reach of the children when the ropes were not in use.

(Coulson, J: 'R v York College, Leeds Crown Court 14 February 2014 Sentencing Remarks of Coulson J' www.judiciary.gov.uk

 For the agenda

Why is following health and safety procedures so important in your business?

 Back to the team

- Are challenging play opportunities putting children at risk?
- How are we teaching children to manage risks?

Asphyxiation

Audit your setting:

Plan	
	Think about how you are going to manage health and safety in *your* setting, what you want to achieve in terms of health and safety and what procedures you need to put in place.
	What resources are required to put your plan into action?
	Clearly define staff responsibilities and define who is responsible for what. This can be done by name or job title.
	Identify and prioritise what needs to be done first through risk assessment
	Don't forget to consider activities such as sleeping when completing your risk assessments..
Do	
	Tell staff what their responsibilities are and ensure that they understand them.
	Provide information, instruction, training and supervision so that staff can do their job properly and that they are competent.
	Provide training based on evaluation of training needs.
	Evaluate what impact the training has had.
	Select equipment that is fit for purpose.
	Ensure that manufacturers' instructions are followed when assembling equipment.
	Check correct assembly/installation of equipment before use.
Check	
	Establish that staff understand their responsibilities and what is expected by talking to them.
	Use workplace inspections and audit to check that health and safety procedures are being followed and that control measures are effective.
	Is there a procedure for reporting, recording and investigating any accidents or near misses?
	Investigate accidents and incidents. Remember, it is not a blame game. It is about prevention. Accident and incidents will have a number of causes. You need to identify them all and get to the root cause.
	Make sure that health and safety is on the agenda for team meetings and supervision.
	Check for product recalls to ensure resources and equipment continue to be safe and suitable.
Act	
	Evaluate and review risk assessments.
	Measure your health and safety performance.
	Act on the lessons that you have learned.

Common elements shared by case files

The case files we have looked at in this chapter share similar weaknesses that contributed to the tragic outcomes. These are outlined below:

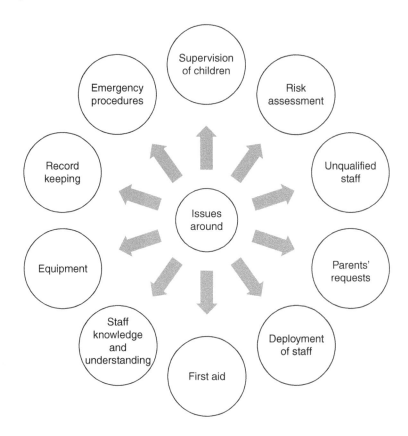

Weaknesses in any one of these issues has the potential to result in consequences. However, our analysis highlights that it was a combination of factors that resulted in each individual tragedy. It is interesting to note that all of the issues are connected to failures associated with leadership and management.

For the agenda

Revisit the cases in this chapter, considering your setting's personal values of:

- working safely
- being responsible and accountable for actions
- caring for others' safety
- reporting all accidents and near misses
- speaking up if you see poor practice/unsafe behaviour
- being a good role model.

Safety campaigns

Various campaigns have been established to try and educate people about the risks of asphyxiation and prevent further tragedies. These include:

Choking

- www.sja.org.uk

Nappy sacks

- www.rospa.com/homesafety
- www.makeitsafe.org.uk

Blind cords

- www.capt.org.uk

Button batteries

- www.rospa.com/homesafety
- www.capt.org.uk
- www.newcastle.gov.uk

We also remember

Since 2000, the following children have also died in day care settings due to asphyxiation.

Name and age	Year of death	Nature of death	More information
Jake Wiseman, aged 3 years	2005	Choked on a meatball at lunchtime in nursery	www.news.bbc.co.uk, article entitled 'Child choked to death on meatball'. Published: 2005/12/09 16:04:57 GMT © BBC
Katie Stockham, aged 4 years	2005	Choked on a piece of cake	www.news.bbc.co.uk/1, article entitled 'Nursery pupil dies after choking'. Published: 2005/09/06 17:16:22 GMT © BBC
Adam Milner, aged 2 years	2009	Choked on a sausage that had been cut up for him for his lunch	www.telegraph.co.uk, article entitled 'Child died choking on a sausage at nursery'. Published: 05 Mar 2011 8:00AM GMT © Telegraph Media Group Limited
Dylan Dosanjh, aged 4 years	2011	Choked on a grape after eating his lunch	www.coventrytelegraph.net/news, article entitled 'Coventry school staff's fight to save four-year-old who choked to death'. Published: 3 October 2011, 07:35AM GMT by Coventry Telegraph © Trinity Mirror Midlands
Tiya Chauhan, aged 22 months	2012	Choked on a jelly cube that had been put into the free flow play area	www.nurseryworld.co.uk, article entitled 'Nursery found "grossly negligent" by inquest into child death'. Published: 05 September 2014, by Catherine Gaunt © Nursery World: MA Education
Millie Thompson, aged 9 months	2012	Choked on the mashed potato of a shepherd's pie she was being fed for lunch	www.bbc.co.uk, article entitled 'Millie Thompson death: Coroner's first aid training plea'. Published: 5 December 2013 © BBC
Chantelle Firth, aged 6 years	2012	Choked on food at lunchtime	www.dailymail.co.uk, article entitled 'Tragedy at primary school as girl, six, dies after "choking on her lunch" by Jill Reilly. © Associated Newspapers Ltd, the Daily Mail, The Mail on Sunday & Metro Media Group
Isabel Pearce, aged 13 years	2015	Choked on a meatball at lunchtime	www.dailymail.co.uk, article entitled 'Girl, 13, who choked to death on meatball from her school canteen' by Gemma Mullin. © Associated Newspapers Ltd, the Daily Mail, The Mail on Sunday & Metro Media Group

4 Crushing/Compression

Definition of crushing/compression

Crush: 'Deform, pulverize, or force inwards by compressing forcefully' (Oxford English Dictionary).

Compress: 'Flatten by pressure; squeeze or press' (Oxford English Dictionary).

Case File 1: Rhiya Malin, aged 2 years

Date and nature of death: 7 November 2007. Rhiya Malin suffered a heart attack due to compression of her neck, after her head became trapped inside a wooden playhouse.

Location: Eton Manor Day Nursery, Chigwell, Essex

Chelmsford Crown Court verdict: Casterbridge Care and Education and Casterbridge Nurseries (Eton Manor) admitted the breach. Nursery Manager Karen Jacobs was cleared by the jury. Staff member Kayley Murphy was found guilty of failing to provide adequate care.

Enforcement outcome: The companies were fined £150,000 between them with £70,000 costs. Kayley Murphy was fined £2,400.

(Source: www.bbc.co.uk/news/uk-england-essex-23100844, article entitled 'Rhiya Malin death: Nursery firms and care worker fined', by BBC News. Published: 28 June 2013 © Copyright of BBC News).

Background details

Rhiya was not observed going into the playhouse in the outside area of Eton Manor Day Nursery. A member of staff (Kayley Murphy), who should have been supervising the children playing outside, was found to be talking on her mobile phone. When all the children were brought inside at the end of the play session it was noted that Rhiya was missing. Rhiya was found hanging in the playhouse with her head trapped between the wall and the roof of the playhouse.

Contributing factors with links to the EYFS

- **Lack of supervision:** Despite there being four members of staff outside with the children, Rhiya was able to go into the playhouse unnoticed and was not missed until all the children were brought back inside. No one saw her and no one heard her. The EYFS framework 3.28 outlines that staffing arrangements must meet the needs of all children and that children must always be within sight and hearing of staff.

- **Staff distracted, as using mobile phone while on duty:** By using her phone on duty, it is clear that the member of staff was distracted and not as alert or vigilant as would be expected for the outdoor supervision of children. The EYFS framework 3.4 links the use of mobile phones in settings to safeguarding children. At an inspection, this type of behaviour could impact on the judgement for the contribution of the early years provision to children's well-being. 'Not all practitioners have sufficient knowledge and/or they are not vigilant enough to ensure that children are kept safe and safeguarded and that their health and welfare are promoted' (Ofsted, Early years inspection handbook, May 2015, No. 102101 www.gov.uk).

- **Policies and procedures ignored by staff:** Kayley Murphy chose to blatantly disregard the nursery's policies and procedures regarding the use of mobile phones. Indeed, staff gave evidence at the trial that this practice was commonplace among most other staff, even though they knew that this behaviour was unacceptable. This indicates a clear shortfall between expectations and practice. Having written documentation in place is insufficient: staff need to be committed to implementing policies and procedures and senior managements need to be persuasive and consistent in monitoring staff performance and sanctioning non-compliance. This helps to establish a culture of safety within the setting and forms part of the judgement at inspection for leadership and management: 'how well safe practices and a culture of safety are promoted and understood' (Ofsted, Early years inspection handbook, May 2015, No. 102101 www.gov.uk).

- **Lack of professionalism as staff behaved differently if managers present:** Staff admitted during the trial that they behaved differently if managers were present, but when they were unsupervised by management they disregarded the rule about the use of mobile phones. This type of behaviour may contribute to an inadequate judgement at inspection when evaluating the effectiveness of leadership and management of the early years provision: 'Management and accountability arrangements are not clear or are not understood by providers and/or their managers' (Ofsted, Early years inspection handbook, May 2015, No.102101 www.gov.uk).

- **The playhouse had been modified and a revised risk assessment was not undertaken:** The playhouse had been bought by the nursery and the roof had been modified to prevent it from blowing off. Staff then failed to undertake a risk assessment on this piece of equipment, which may have posed additional hazards as a result of the modification. The EYFS framework 3.64 highlights the requirement to comply with other legislation, including risk assessment and health and safety.

- **Manufacturer's instructions regarding supervision were ignored:** The instructions stated that the playhouse was suitable for children aged between two and six years, but that there should always be adult supervision when children were using the playhouse.

Contributing factors with links to the CCR/VCR

CR 1.8 Welfare of the children being cared for
CR 5.5 Suitability and safety of premises and equipment

Contributing factors under Health and Safety

- The presence of a trapping point between the wall and ceiling of the Wendy house.
- Failure by staff to provide adequate supervision during play.
- Actions by staff during periods when supervision should be provided, for example use of mobile phones.
- Manufacturer's instructions ignored.

A lack of an effective health and safety management system:

- A failure to undertake a risk assessment on equipment before taking it into use.
- A failure to ensure that staff provided adequate supervision in the garden.
- A failure to deal with bad practice such as the use of mobile phones by staff during working hours.

Legislation breached

A charge was laid against the provider for a breach of Section 3(1) of the Health and Safety at Work Etc. Act 1974. The offence for failing to meet this duty is detailed in Section 33(1)(a) of the Act. Charges were also brought against the Nursery Manager, Karen Jacobs, and Kayley Murphy, a member of staff. Employees have a duty under Section 7 (a) of the Health and Safety at Work Etc. Act 1974 to take reasonable care of their own health and safety and that of others.

'It shall be the duty of every employee while at work to take reasonable care for the health and safety of himself and of other persons who may be affected by his acts or omissions at work.'[1]

Key point ⊶O

- Health and safety procedures are only effective if staff follow them.

---

[1] Page [49] extract from [Health and Safety at Work Etc. Act 1974] © Crown Copyright – Use subject to Open Government Licence v3.0 [http://www.nationalarchives.gov.uk/doc/open-government-licence/version/3/] – Except where otherwise stated.

Crushing/Compression

Judge's comments

Judge Walden-Smith said:

'I do not find that the companies were placing profit above safety but health and safety were not being taken seriously enough. Necessary support to staff was not given to enable health and safety to be given the prominence it required.'

'She was very young and therefore highly vulnerable and, while this is not a public company providing public services in which safety is entrusted, the business was a nursery where the care of the children is paramount and where parents have placed the ultimate trust, the care of their child.'

'The companies failed in their core obligation.'

Of the nursery assistant she said:

'She failed on that day to properly supervise the children for whom she was responsible as the room manager and she used her mobile phone.'

'She failed to direct those working with and under her direction to spread themselves across the garden, and she joined with them in congregating in one place in order to have a social chat.'

(Walden-Smith, K. www.dailymail.co.uk)

Reflection

- Do you challenge health and safety violations and unsafe behaviour?

- Do staff understand what you mean by unsafe behaviour?
- Do you manage safety with the same emphasis as you manage other aspects of your setting?
- Are staff consistent in their day-to-day management of health and safety?

- What action do you take to deal with health and safety violations and unsafe behaviour?
- Evaluate and review health and safety policies and procedures.
- Plan peer observation to monitor consistency.

 Back to the team

Ask staff to identify what they think are health and safety violations and unsafe behaviours.

For the agenda

Do you have safety conversations with your staff?

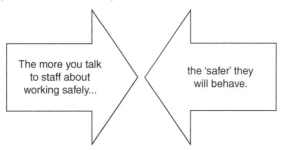

The more you talk to staff about working safely...

the 'safer' they will behave.

 # Back to the team

Audit your setting:

Plan	
	Identify and prioritise what needs to be done first through risk assessment.
	How will you show your commitment to health and safety?
	Think about how you will ascertain staff knowledge and commitment to safety as part of your recruitment processes.
	Plan how you will develop a culture of safety in your setting.
Do	
	Have clear sanctions about consequences for not following policies and procedures, and implement sanctions consistently.
	Be personally involved in safety management.
	Get to know your staff. Use one-to-one sessions and supervision to ascertain understanding and identify training needs.
Check	
	Check that all staff understand their responsibilities with regard to supervising children: make your expectations clear.
	Make sure that staff follow assembly instructions and guidelines when using toys and equipment.
Act	
	If you see unacceptable practice or staff behaving unsafely in your setting, intervene. Do not allow poor practice to become a habit or the norm.

Safety campaigns

'Gate Safe'. RoSPA campaign regarding electric gates:

- www.rospa.com

Ongoing safety campaigns organised by CAPT:

- www.capt.org.uk

We also remember

Name and age	Year of death	Nature of death	More information
Oliver Ladwa, aged 2 years	2006	Crushed by an ambulance that accidently rolled down a hill. The ambulance was visiting the playgroup.	http://news.bbc.co.uk http://news.bbc.co.uk/1/hi/england/london/6599825.stm , article entitled 'Boy ambulance death "accidental"' by BBC News. Published: 2007/04/27 16:24:28 GMT © Copyright of BBC

5 Allergic reactions

Definition of allergic reactions

An allergen is a substance which, when it comes into contact with the body, produces a damaging immune response. An allergic response can happen after:

- touching
- tasting
- eating
- breathing in a substance.

There are many different types of allergens. Some common things that people may be allergic to include certain types of food, plants, animal hair/fur, pollen, dust, latex and insect stings. Allergens are important because of the way that they affect the person who is sensitised to them. The effects can range from mild, moderate to severe symptoms. Examples of mild symptoms include sneezing, runny nose, watering eyes, coughing and a localised area of itchy skin. However, in some cases the response by the immune system can be life threatening. Acute effects – such as swelling of the eyes, lips, hands and feet, difficulty in breathing, skin rash, collapse or loss of consciousness – occur rapidly. In certain circumstances if these effects go untreated the person can die. This acute reaction is known as **anaphylaxis**.

A food allergy is the body's reaction in terms of an immune response to a normally harmless food. These foods are usually proteins such as fish, milk and eggs. The body's immune system, which normally protects us against disease and infection, treats these proteins in the food as a threat. This triggers the allergic response. There is no cure for food allergies, although some young children may grow out of certain allergies such as milk and eggs. Most food allergies are managed by avoiding the food that causes the allergy. In the food industry, food allergies and food intolerance are important issues not only for the final consumer of the product but also for any business such as a nursery that provides meals or food for clients. The tragic death of Thomas Egan illustrates the importance of knowing what ingredients are in food and the tragic consequences of making a mistake.

Key point ⚬━O

- Food allergies can kill!

Statistics

The Food Standards Agency (FSA) estimates that:

- 21 million people in the UK suffer from at least one type of allergy
- up to 8% of children and 2% of adults are diagnosed with a food allergy
- at least 1 in 100 people have coeliac disease.

Food allergy and food intolerance have been increasing and, given the scale of the problem, research is being undertaken to identify the causes of the increase. In the UK it is estimated that ten people die per year of food allergies from anaphylaxis. In addition there are 1,500 asthma deaths, which may be linked to food allergy as many people with a food allergy also suffer from asthma. Teenagers and young people appear to be particularly at risk. Those suffering a reaction may or may not know that they have a food allergy (FSA, http://allergytraining.food.gov.uk/english/food-allergy-facts.aspx).

Changes in the law

Consumer law changed on 13 December 2014. The new law is based on the EU Food Information for Consumers Regulation (No. 1169/2011). It lays down rules for the new requirements and 'aims to achieve a high level of health for consumers and to guarantee their right to information'. The new requirements are enforced through the Food Information Regulations 2014 and other equivalent regulations for Northern Ireland, Scotland and Wales. The Regulations have brought about certain changes:

There are the 14 foods that appear on the EU list of major allergens:

- Celery
- Cereals containing gluten
- Crustaceans
- Eggs
- Fish
- Lupin
- Milk
- Molluscs (shellfish)
- Mustard
- Tree nuts such as: almonds, brazil nuts, hazelnuts, walnuts
- Peanuts

- Sesame seeds
- Soya
- Sulphites

Key points ⚊O

- If you are a setting that provides meals or snacks then you are a food business operator under the terms of food safety law. You have a legal duty to provide food that is safe to eat.
- For food businesses, including restaurants, schools, cafés, nurseries etc. where food is being prepared or supplied for sale, information on the 14 key allergens present in food or ingredients in food must be available and provided on request. This means that it is essential that the provider knows what is in their food. They must read the ingredients on any pre-packed foods that are used and check to see if they are allergenic foods on the list or contain any of the 14 key allergens as ingredients.
- It is also important to consider how the food is prepared, for example cooked in groundnut oil (which contains peanuts), and also any garnishes that may be used, for example sesame seeds.
- The new law has also brought about some changes and improvements in the labelling of pre-packed food to help with this. For pre-packed foods, the list of ingredients is regulated so that it can be read and understood easily. The 14 key allergens will need to be highlighted if used as ingredients in the food. These foods may be obviously present (e.g. fish) or they may be in food as an ingredient, for example anchovies (fish) and malt vinegar (barley) in Worcestershire sauce. They may be an additive in food – for example, sulphur dioxide in wine appears as 'sulphites' on the label.
- The 14 major allergens detailed on the EU list must be emphasised on the ingredients list. They need to be emphasised clearly in bold print, underlined or in a contrasting text colour with a clear reference to the allergen name as it appears on the EU list.

Where to go for help on food allergens

The FSA's website has lots of useful information to help a business to manage this requirement. An advisory leaflet regarding the new regulations, entitled 'Allergen Information for Loose Foods: Advice on the new Food Information Regulations for Small and Medium Food Businesses', is available to download on the FSA website at: www.food.

gov.uk There is also a similar leaflet that explains the law relating to pre-packed foods and allergens. This is available at: www.food.gov.uk

A helpful checklist that illustrates the sort of questions that an Enforcement Officer might ask during a food safety inspection about food allergens and how they are controlled is available at: https://www.food.gov.uk It is also important to remember that children may be allergic to other foods not included on the EU list. A provider needs to take account of this and discuss specific issues with parents or guardians. They must ensure that there is a system in place for this information to be disseminated to staff and for the risk to the allergy sufferer to be controlled. Training staff in allergy awareness is essential. There is a free training course available online via the FSA website at: www.food.gov.uk

Information about food allergy alerts and product withdrawals due to allergy contamination or incorrect allergen labelling is available at: https://www.food.gov.uk Other useful organisations providing information about food allergy/intolerance and asthma are:

- www.allergyuk.org
- www.anaphylaxis.org.uk
- www.coeliac.org.uk/home/
- www.asthma.org.uk/advice-nursery-and-childcare

Case File 1: Thomas Egan, aged 5 months

Date and nature of death: 11 April 2002, due to an allergic reaction after being fed a milk product
Location: Jigsaw Day Nursery, Milton Keynes
Inquest verdict: Accidental death contributed to by neglect (by the nursery).
Crown Court verdict: Jigsaw Day Nurseries Ltd pleaded guilty.
Enforcement outcome: The nursery was fined £60,000 plus £19,000 costs.
(Source: www.news.bbc.co.uk/1/hi/england/beds/bucks/herts/3226675.stm ,
article entitled 'Baby death nursery fined', by BBC News. Published: Thursday,
30 October, 2003, 12:47 GMT © Copyright of BBC News).

Background details

Thomas Egan attended Jigsaw Day Nursery in Milton Keynes. He was allergic to all dairy products. Thomas' mother had informed the nursery of her son's allergy in order for the nursery to devise a suitable care plan and be alert to his specific dietary requirements. However, a nursery nurse fed Thomas a breakfast cereal without checking the food label. The cereal contained dried milk. Thomas died from massive anaphylactic shock.

Contributing factors with links to the EYFS

- **Special dietary requirements for Thomas disregarded/not understood by all staff:** Thomas was fed a breakfast cereal that contained dried milk. The member of staff who fed Thomas had not checked the food label. The EYFS framework 3.47 states that any special dietary needs must be part of the admission procedures. It also requires providers to act upon advice and guidance from parents about their child's specific dietary needs. It is worth ensuring that all staff understand food labels and that even substances that are dried can prove fatal to a child, as in this case.

- **Issues around staff training and support:** There was clearly a communication issue in this particular case as the member of staff was not aware or did not understand Thomas' specific needs. This information needs to be accessible to all staff who may be feeding and caring for children. The EYFS framework 3.20 and 3.21 cover staff qualifications, training, support and skills.

- **Issues around key person:** The key person role is to ensure that children are given individualised care in conjunction with close working with parents and/or carers. This particular tragedy could have been prevented if staff had read the ingredients on the cereal packet and if Thomas' specific needs had been risk assessed and all staff been made aware. The EYFS framework 1.10 and 3.27 cover key persons.

Key point ⚷

- Weaknesses in the key person system could contribute to a judgement of inadequate at inspection. 'The key person system is not well embedded. Care practices do not support all children's emotional well-being and welfare, with some children failing to form secure attachments with their carers' (Ofsted, Early years inspection handbook, May 2015, p14, No.102101. www.gov.uk).

Contributing factors with links to the CCR/VCR

CR 4.3 Qualifications and training (CCR only)

Contributing factors under Health and Safety

- Anaphylactic shock caused by an allergy to milk. Thomas was fed a breakfast cereal that was found to contain skimmed milk powder.
- A member of staff failed to recognise that the cereal product contained milk protein.
- The member of staff failed to check the label on the product.
- There was confusion among staff regarding the extent of Thomas' food allergy.
- A failure to complete risk assessments on children with allergies.
- A lack of an effective health and safety management system to control risks to children with allergies.
- A failure to follow instructions given by a parent in relation to their child's allergy and to communicate this information effectively to staff.
- A failure to train staff in the importance of reading food labels.

(Source: www.standard.co.uk/news/nursery-admits-guilt-over-baby-death-6986169. html , article entitled 'Nursery admits guilt over baby death', by Nilufer Atik. Published: 08 August 2003 00.00 BST © Copyright of the Evening Standard).

Legislation breached

Failure to meet the general duty of an employer to 'persons not in their employment' under Section 3(1) of the Health and Safety at Work Etc. Act 1974:
'It shall be the duty of every employer to conduct his undertaking in such a way as to ensure, so far as is reasonably practicable, that persons not in his employment who may be affected thereby are not thereby exposed to risks to their health or safety.'[1] The offence for failing to meet this duty is detailed in Section 33(1) (a) of the Act.

Judge's comments

Judge Christopher Tyrer said: 'At the root of this appalling tragedy, one fact seems to me to stand clear, that this death was preventable. That, I expect, is the most anguishing factor for Mr and Mrs Egan.' He added: 'What happened was preventable and should have been prevented. That's the gravity of this prosecution in my mind' (Tyrer, C. www.independent. co.uk/news/uk/this-britain/nursery-is-fined-60000-over-death-of-allergic-baby-93930. html).

For the agenda

How do we recognise signs of an allergy and how should we deal with an allergic reaction in an emergency situation?

Dealing with an allergic reaction

It is important that you and your staff know what to do if someone has a severe allergic reaction, as this is a medical emergency. Children with allergies can react to insect stings immediately, therefore needing prompt medical intervention.

Children can be allergic to rubber latex. It is worth remembering that latex can be found in:

- balloons
- rubber bands
- carpet backing
- furniture fillings
- disposable gloves.

It can sometimes be difficult to tell whether it is a severe allergic reaction or whether the symptoms are being caused by another serious condition. Look for the warning signs.

Severe symptoms of anaphylaxis

Warning signs are shown below:

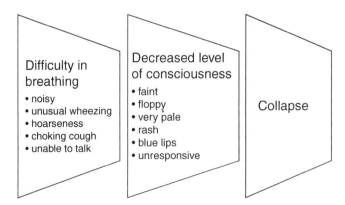

- Do not move the person.
- Call 999 and explain that you believe that someone is having a severe allergic reaction (say 'anna-fill-axis'). Ask for an ambulance with a paramedic to be sent.
- Send someone outside to wait for the ambulance and to direct the paramedics inside when they arrive.
- Ask the casualty if they have an auto-injector (EpiPen).
- Help them to retrieve it.
- It is always best if they can self-administer. (A young child may not be able to do this.)
- If they are unable to do so, you or your first aider can offer to assist them, provided you know what to do and have been trained.
- Dealing with the casualty is the priority.
- However, remember to investigate what happened. Record what food was eaten.
- Review your food safety management procedures.

Be confident about using an EpiPen

Ensure that staff access training on how to administer an EpiPen.

- EpiPens can be given through clothing, but avoid pockets, seams, folds.
- Check the expiry date.
- Check the contents through the viewing window. The liquid adrenaline should be clear and colourless.

- EpiPens are light sensitive. Keep in a dark place, but do not refrigerate.
- Use an EpiPen when you need to – children having an allergic reaction are more at risk from the reaction than from the EpiPen.

> ## Key point ⚬━O
>
> - Remember, if adrenaline is given early on, there will be a better outcome for the child.

Children with asthma

Working in partnership with parents and/or carers is crucial when dealing with children with asthma. Parents will want to be reassured that their child can be cared for and dealt with promptly in the event of an asthma attack.

 ## Back to the team

- Do you have an asthma policy in your setting?
- Do you know what triggers specific children's asthma?
- How would you deal with a child having an asthma attack?
- Where are the children's inhalers kept? Are they locked away or easily accessible?
- When did you last check expiry dates on any inhalers you may have in your setting?
- Is everyone clear about what to do in the event of an emergency and who to contact?

> ## Key point ⚬━O
>
> - Remember, asthma exacerbates allergic reactions. Children with asthma have a higher risk of having a severe or anaphylactic reaction.

Reflection

- Consider how children's allergies influence your planning.

- Do you consider children's allergies when you put items into the role-play/free-flow play areas?
- Do you assess the potential for cross-contamination hazards in your setting?

- Review and evaluate your planning. Think about items that you may put into the role-play or free-flow areas that may trigger children's asthma.

 Back to the team

Audit your setting:

Plan	
	Aim to be a proactive manager when organising children's admissions. Outstanding leadership and management ensures 'Children's needs are quickly identified and exceptionally well met through highly effective partnerships between the setting, parents, external agencies and other providers' (Ofsted, Evaluation schedule for inspections of registered early years provision, August 2014, No. 120086).
	Think about your admission procedures. Does your documentation ask enough questions about children' specific needs?
	Identify and prioritise what needs to be done through risk assessment.
	Think about how the environment will be kept clean from food allergens.
	Your food safety management system should include how you will manage food allergens.
	Plan the systems you need to have in place for dealing with children with food allergies or food intolerance.
	What training have you given your staff in food allergies?
	Would you and your staff know how to deal with a child who suffered a severe allergic reaction as a result of eating your food?

Do	
	Discuss with staff the need to liaise very closely with children's parents and carers to devise individualised care plans for each child.
	Keep lists of ingredients of foods not to be given to specific children and ensure that all staff, including students, are aware.
	Include allergy awareness as part of staff training programmes.
	Train staff involved in food handling and feeding to read food product labels.
	Make sure that you comply with the requirements of the Food Information Regulations and log the presence of the 14 food allergens present in your menu items. You can use a menu tracker to do this.
	Ensure easy access to emergency medicines.
	Train your first aiders in the use of EpiPens or auto-injectors.
	Make your staff are aware of how to deal with allergies, including spotting the symptoms.
Check	
	Make sure that all staff, especially key workers, are aware of children's specific needs and that they know how to care for them and who to seek advice from.
	Check that staff are trained to administer emergency medicines and that their training is up to date.
	How well are food allergies being managed in your setting?
	That both you and your staff know where to look for allergen ingredient information on pre-packed foods.
	Make sure that you and your staff are checking your pre-packed foods to see what food allergens they may contain.
	What happens if you need to substitute an ingredient or use a different brand?
	Are you being systematic and thorough in recording, keeping and reviewing your allergy ingredient information?
	Check information about ingredients from your food supplier.
	Have you investigated any allergy incidents or near misses?
Act	
	Use supervision sessions to ensure staff are providing individualised care for every child.
	Have you had any allergy incidents or near misses? What have you learned from the investigation or from incidents at similar premises?
	What do you need to change?
	Have you actioned any results of internal/external audits or enforcement inspections?
	Remember: risk management is a continuous process. It needs to be reviewed.

Safety campaigns and research

More guidance on up-to-date information on allergies and asthma is available here:
Allergies: www.allergyuk.org
Anaphylaxis: www.anaphylaxis.org.uk
Asthma: www.asthma.org.uk
Coeliac: www.coeliac.org.uk

6 Finger trapping

Definition of a finger trap accident

Trap: 'Have (something, typically a part of the body) held tightly by something so that it cannot be freed' (Oxford English Dictionary).

A finger trap accident could result in:

- crushing
- bruising
- fractures
- amputation.

Finger trap accidents always result in significant pain and distress for the child and, sometimes, years of medical intervention/corrective surgery. This is particularly disturbing, as this type of accident is preventable.

Statistics

According to RoSPA, 'it is estimated that 15,000 children trap their fingers in doors in the home each year in the UK' (RoSPA Position Statements, September 2014). Our research has revealed that day care settings also contain entrapment hazards, such as classroom doors, toilet doors, cubicle doors, cupboards etc. This, coupled with the diverse age range in a group of children, their specific needs and variables in behaviour, means finger entrapment poses a huge risk to children in childcare settings.

Case File 1: Boy, aged 14 months

Date and nature of injury: 14 October 2009, severed fingertip
Location: Just Learning Nursery, Thorpe St Andrew, Norwich
Cambridge Crown Court verdict: Just Learning Ltd admitted the breach.
Enforcement outcome: The nursery was fined £40,000 and costs of £35,000.
(Source: www.bbc.co.uk/news/uk-england-norfolk-16288570 , article entitled 'Nursery fined after boy's fingertip severed by closing door', by BBC News Norfolk. Published: 21 December 2011 © Copyright of BBC News).

Background details

Just Learning Limited had previously been fined £67,000 plus £78,000 costs in 2009 as Georgia Hollick had choked to death in 2006 at one of their nurseries. In this case, the boy had been playing by a kitchen door when the little finger on his left hand became trapped in the door. Delays in dealing with the accident meant that surgeons could not re-attach the fingertip. Judge Jacobs said the incident had been handled in a 'less than satisfactory way'. He also drew similarities with failings in the Georgia Hollick case and said 'it was a fallacy that issues raised at the previous case had been remedied'.

Contributing factors with links to the EYFS

- **Risk assessment:** Failings in risk assessment contributed to the death of Georgia Hollick in 2006. A thorough risk assessment in this instance would have identified the risk of finger trapping when assessing the doors and the age range of children playing in the area. The EYFS framework 3.64 states that 'risk assessments should identify aspects of the environment that need to be checked on a regular basis, when and by whom those aspects will be checked, and how the risk will be removed or minimised' (DfE, Statutory Framework for the EYFS, 2014, p28).

- **Finger guards:** While there is no requirement within the EYFS for providers to install finger guards, it is clear in this case that they would have prevented this accident. The purpose of the safeguarding and welfare requirements of the EYFS framework is to ensure children are cared for and educated in high quality, safe and welcoming settings, where they can grow in confidence and become motivated learners. The EYFS framework 3.2 states that 'providers must take all necessary steps to keep children safe and well' (DfE, Statutory Framework for the EYFS, 2014, p16).

- **Lack of understanding regarding the developmental needs of babies:** Babies, especially, like to explore their environment and repeat movements. This helps to develop their coordination and control. They are usually fascinated with opening and closing doors either on cupboards or the main doors in rooms. It is imperative that staff can adjust their expectations regarding children's levels of curiosity as they develop. The EYFS framework 1.6 states that 'practitioners must consider the individual needs, interests, and stage of development of each child in their care' (DfE, Statutory Framework for the EYFS, 2014, p8).

- For more information on child development, see here for early years outcomes guidance: www.gov.uk

Contributing factors with links to the CCR/VCR

CR 4.3 Qualifications and training (CCR only)
CR 5.5 Suitability and safety of premises and equipment

Contributing factors under Health and Safety

- Entrapment hazard on the door to the milk kitchen.

- Management failure to recognise and assess the risk of entrapment and, as a consequence, failure to fit finger guards to doors accessed by children.

- Finger guards were fitted retrospectively on doors on site and throughout the other nurseries across the company's estate.

- Management failure to act on a recognised and known risk: the risk of injury to children through trapping their fingers in doors was well known, the consequences of any accident potentially severe and the chance of injury was high.

Judge Peter Jacobs said that all nurseries should ensure that door guards were fitted at their premises as a matter of course and said: 'Every local authority should send out a directive to every single nursery to put up door guards and told that if not, they are committing an offence and could be taken to magistrates court and fined.' He said that there was an obvious risk of children getting their fingers caught in doors and said: 'The doors should have been safeguarded so as to ensure the entrapment of children's fingers did not take place.' He added that nurseries which cared for young children had an 'enormous responsibility' (Jacobs, P. www.whtimes.co.uk/news/70_000_fine_costs_for_norwich_nursery_where_ youngster_had_part_of_finger_chopped_off_1_1159715 Welwyn Hatfield Times article entitled '£70,000 fine, costs for Norwich nursery where youngster had part of finger chopped off.' Published 21 December 2011 15.55 © Welwyn and Hatfield Times).

Legislation breached

Failure to meet the general duty of an employer to 'persons not in their employment' under Section 3(1) of the Health and Safety at Work Etc. Act 1974:
'It shall be the duty of every employer to conduct his undertaking in such a way as to ensure, so far as is reasonably practicable, that persons not in his employment who may be affected thereby are not thereby exposed to risks to their health or safety.'[1]

(Source: www.whtimes.co.uk/news/70_000_fine_costs_for_norwich_nursery_where_ youngster_had_part_of_finger_chopped_off _1_1159715).

Key point ⚬━O

- The installation of suitable, approved finger guards, correctly installed, would have prevented this accident, and while the child has not suffered significant cosmetic disfiguration, he has lost the feeling in the tip of his finger.

[1]Page [67] extract from [Health and Safety at Work Etc. Act 1974] © Crown Copyright – Use subject to Open Government Licence v3.0 [http://www.nationalarchives.gov.uk/doc/open-government-licence/version/3/] – Except where otherwise stated.

Finger trapping

Environmental Health Officer's comments

James Windsor, an Environmental Health Officer with Broadlands Council, said: 'This prosecution is a timely reminder to other nurseries that they should look regularly at their safety procedures and regimes to make sure they are up to standard' (Windsor, J. http://www.bbc.co.uk/news/uk-england-norfolk-16288570).

Reflection

As a result of this accident, Just Learning Limited said it had always accepted its accountability and had subsequently fitted finger guards to all of its nurseries.

- How often do you discuss/evaluate your safety procedures?

- Think about the finger trap hazards in your setting. How many accidents/near misses have there been?
- Does your setting have finger guards fitted, who fitted them and how often are they maintained and checked for suitability?

- Set a goal, to discuss and evaluate health and safety systems.
- Have safety systems as a regular agenda item and supervision prompt.

 For the agenda

- How do we prevent finger trap accidents in our setting?
- Are the systems good enough? How do we know?

Sometimes, in an effort to prevent accidents, settings can be misled by safety products that are not fit for purpose. Some products devised to prevent finger entrapment have been found to be cosmetic only in their capacity to prevent accidents and indeed have increased the risks of accidents to children.

Key point

- Always ensure that your efforts to address potential hazards are not inadvertently creating new ones.

Safety campaigns and research

For good advice on door safety, see the Children's Charter (CSA) Door Safety Standard (DSS):

- www.childrens-charter.org

This includes:

- using door safety specialists to undertake risk assessments
- having approved products, fitted, maintained and regularly inspected to ensure they are fit for purpose
- having a DSS compliance certificate with an expiry date.

Lessons learned for the future

 Back to the team

Health and safety is everyone's responsibility.

Keep alert for potential risks and hazards

Plan	
	Identify aspects of the setting where finger entrapments could occur and prioritise what needs to be done through risk assessment.
Do	
	Discuss with staff the need to be vigilant when supervising children.
Check	
	Ensure that all staff understand the changing developmental needs of the children they are caring for.
Act	
	. . . if you witness dangerous activities/behaviour.
	. . . to ensure that risks are removed or minimised.
	. . . to ensure safety devices are regularly maintained.

Case File 2: Boy, aged 9 years

Date and nature of injury: 11 September 2012, amputation of index finger to the left hand

Location: A special needs school run by Birtenshaw charity

Trafford Magistrate's Court verdict: The defendant pleaded guilty.

Enforcement outcome: Conditional discharge and payment of prosecution costs of £898.00
(Source: www.press.hse.gov.uk/2014/bolton-charity-in-court-after-child-loses-finger-in-school-door/, article entitled 'Bolton charity in court after child loses finger in school door', by HSE. Published: 11 April 2014 © Copyright of HSE)

Background details

The Birtenshaw charity in the North West was given a conditional discharge and ordered to pay prosecution costs by magistrates following a case taken by the HSE. This followed an investigation into an accident where a nine-year-old boy with autism lost a finger when his left hand became trapped in the hinged side of a school door.

The accident took place at the charity's new special needs school. During construction of the new building, the need to fit finger guards to the doors had been identified but the guards were not in place when the school was opened and occupied for use.

Contributing factors with links to the EYFS

This case does not fall into the remit of the EYFS framework because of the age of the child. However, we felt it was important to include this case to highlight the vulnerability of all children, particularly those with special educational needs and/or disabilities.

Contributing factors with links to the CCR/VCR

CR 1.1 Welfare of the children being cared for
CR 5.1 Suitability and safety of premises and equipment

Contributing factors under Health and Safety

- Entrapment hazard on the hinged side of the door to the quiet room.
- Failure to implement an identified control measure to minimise a risk of injury.
- Management failure to check (monitor) that the control measures, i.e. the fitting of finger guards, had been implemented across the site before the occupation of the building by pupils. A number of doors were found not to have finger guards in place.

HSE Inspector's comments

HSE Inspector David Norton said:

'A nine-year-old boy has suffered an injury that will affect him for the rest of his life because of the failings of the charity, which runs the school. 'Birtenshaw knew there was a risk of children's fingers becoming trapped in doors as the pupils who attend the school have learning and physical disabilities, making them particularly vulnerable. 'It would have been relatively easy to walk around the school to check all of the doors had been fitted with finger guards before pupils moved into the new building, but the charity failed to do this.' (Norton, D. www.press.hse.gov. uk/2014/bolton-charity-in-courtafter-child-loses-finger-in-school-door/)

Legislation breached

Failure to meet the general duty of an employer to 'persons not in their employment' under Section 3(1) of the Health and Safety at Work Etc. Act 1974:

'It shall be the duty of every employer to conduct his undertaking in such a way as to ensure, so far as is reasonably practicable, that persons not in his employment who may be affected thereby are not thereby exposed to risks to their health or safety.'[2]

Reflection

In this case, the charity failed to meet its duty 'so far as is reasonably practicable' as the need to fit the finger guards had been identified, the risk of injury was well known, the consequences were severe and the chance of injury was high. The fitting of guards to the doors was a reasonable action to take, proportionate to the risk involved.

- Who completes the risk assessments in your setting?
- Do you think all potential hazards are being addressed?

- Do you know what the risk assessment covers?
- Think about a situation when you saw something unsafe. What action did you take?

ACTION

- Ensure that any identified risks are addressed.
- Appoint someone to check that work has been completed and/or risk is removed.

Lessons learned for the future

Think: Plan, Do, Check, Act

Plan	
	Use risk assessment to prioritise what action needs to be taken first.
	Assign responsibility for completion of tasks.
Do	
	Communicate the findings of the risk assessment and ensure that those responsible for completing tasks know what they have to do and when the work is required to be completed.
Check	
	Monitor the progress of the work to ensure that it is completed properly.
Act	
	Use an action plan to monitor and control progress.
	Serious risks need to be acted on and actioned first.

Safety campaigns and research

It is always worth checking for product recalls on websites such as Which? They often include products where defects have become apparent such as pushchairs, toys and equipment:

- www.search.which.co.uk

Children's Charter is a community interest, non-profit-making organisation that aims to protect the rights of children. Children's Charter can assist settings to implement changes to adopt the Door Safety Standard (DSS):

- www.childrens-charter.org
- www.childrens-charter.org

 Back to the team

- Identify a key person on the team to action/research further.
- Set up an alert system for product recalls/safety notifications.
- How will you brief the team about new information?
- Who will check the equipment and implement change?

Finger trapping

We also remember

The following children have suffered as a result of finger trap accidents.

Name and age	Year of injury	Nature of injury	More information
Kaitlin Gregson, aged 5 years	2007	Left ring finger severed	www.nottinghampost.com, article entitled 'Child's finger severed in school fire door' by This is Nottingham. © Nottingham Post; Local World
Mackenzie Miller, aged 8 months	2009	Tip of middle finger severed	www.personalinjuryclaimsbradford.co.uk, article entitled '5-year-old receives compensation for nursery injury' by PIClaimsBradford. © Personal Injury Claims Bradford
Kacie Lumsden, aged 3 years	2012	Top of her right thumb severed	www.dailymail.co.uk, article entitled 'Toddler's thumb is "ripped off at nursery" after it became trapped between a door and a wall while she was playing' by Daily Mail reporter. © Associated Newspapers Ltd, the Daily Mail, The Mail on Sunday & Metro Media Group
Sophie Dedek, aged 9 months	2013	Lost her fingertip during a taster session at nursery	www.dailymail.co.uk, article entitled 'Our daughter's finger was severed in a nursery door, but staff only realised when they found it on the floor' by Eleanor Harding for The Daily Mail. © Associated Newspapers Ltd, the Daily Mail, The Mail on Sunday & Metro Media Group
Robyn McGinty, aged 15 months	2014	Robyn's middle finger became stuck in a door hinge at the nursery and as the door shut it severed the top of her finger off from the base of the nail.	www.dailyrecord.co.uk, article entitled 'Furious couple slam nursery after their 15-month-old daughter has her finger severed' by Robert Fairnie. © Daily Record and Sunday Mail
'A child'	2014	A child trapped their finger in a door and the nursery failed to notify the accident within 14 days.	www.swindonadvertiser.co.uk, article entitled 'Nursery failed to report injury' by Beren Cross © Swindon Advertiser; Newsquest

7 Falls from height

Chapter overview

Definition of falls from height

To fall: 'An event that results in a person coming to rest inadvertently on the ground or floor or other lower level' (The European Child Safety Alliance, Childhood Falls, 2009). Falls from height are usually associated with working in industry –for example, falling from roofs, ladders, scaffolding, machinery and vehicles etc. – and as such are governed by the Work at Height Regulations 2005. In day care setting the risks for children associated with falls from height tend to be around supervision of children and environmental factors, especially during care practices, such as nappy changing or children climbing and then accessing open windows.

Statistics

Data from the HSE around falls from height tend to reflect industry accidents. The Home and Leisure Accident Surveillance web database (HASS/LASS) ceased to collate data relating to accidents in 2002. RoSPA is actively campaigning to re-establish injury data collection in the UK. According to RoSPA, every year more than 4,200 children are involved in falls on the stairs and 4,000 children under the age of 15 are injured falling from windows (www.rospa.com/home-safety/advice/general/facts-and-figures/). According to Childalert research, 39% of all children's accidents are from falling. Ten children die each year from falling through a window or off a balcony (www.childalert.co.uk/safety.php?tab=Safety).

Case File 1: Eshan Ahmed, aged 3 years

Date and nature of injury: 31 March 2011, fractured skull requiring an induced coma for treatment
Location: Little Hippos Multi-Cultural Nursery and Day Care Centre, Birmingham
Birmingham Crown Court verdict: Nursery owner, Irshad Ahmed, pleaded guilty.
Enforcement outcome: £16,000 fine, costs of £7,500 and a £15 victim surcharge
(Source: www.telegraph.co.uk, article entitled 'Nursery fined over cover-up after fall left child in a coma', © Telegraph Media Group Limited).

Background details

Eshan fell head first onto a concrete floor after falling from a 15-foot-high fire escape that was known to be unsafe, due to large gaps in the railings. Witnesses said Eshan dangled by one of his feet before falling through the railings onto the concrete floor below. The owner of the nursery, Irshad Ahmed, knew the fire escape was unsafe, but continued to use it regularly as an entrance and exit. Mr Ahmed lied to Eshan's mother and Ofsted, by saying that her son had been pushed off the fire escape during a routine fire drill. Mr Ahmed also failed to notify the incident within ten days as required under RIDDOR.

Contributing factors with links to the EYFS

- **Safety of premises:** During the proceedings, the court heard that the nursery owner, Irshad Ahmed, knew the fire escape was unsafe, but continued to use it as a means of access and egress. The EYFS framework 3.54 outlines the need for providers to 'ensure that their premises, including overall floor space and outdoor spaces, are fit for purpose and suitable for the age of children cared for' (DfE, Statutory Framework for the EYFS, 2014. p27).

- **Suitability of adults:** The nursery owner fabricated a story around Eshan's accident and tried to get staff to collude with his deception. This brings into question the integrity and professionalism of the nursery owner. It also raises concerns about the culture of safety within this setting and could contribute to an inadequate judgement when evaluating the effectiveness of leadership and management: 'how well safe practices and a culture of safety are promoted and understood' (Ofsted, Early years inspection handbook, May 2015, No 102101 https://www.gov.uk/government/uploads/system/uploads/attachment_data/file/429502/Early_years_inspection_handbook.pdf).

- **Complying with other legislation:** The nursery owner failed in his duty to make the relevant notifications about the accident within relevant timescales. The EYFS framework 3.51 covers the notifications to Ofsted process and the EYFS framework 3.54 covers the requirement for providers to comply with other legislation including health and safety, which includes RIDDOR.

- **Risk assessment:** A risk assessment would have identified that the fire escape had large gaps in the railings that would be considered a risk, especially to small children because they could easily slip through and fall a significant distance to the ground. However, a risk assessment alone will not prevent an accident, as is clear in this case. The nursery owner was aware of the hazards and chose to ignore them. The EYFS framework 3.64 covers risk assessment.

Contributing factors with links to the CCR/VCR

CR 1.1 Welfare of the children being cared for
CR 5.1 Suitability and safety of premises and equipment
CR 5.5 Suitability and safety of premises and equipment
CR 13 Matters affecting the welfare of children

Contributing factors under Health and Safety

- There were large gaps in the railings to the fire escape that allowed Eshan to fall through.

A lack of an effective health and safety management system:

- A failure to identify the risk posed by the use of the fire escape through a suitable and sufficient risk assessment.
- A failure to take action to deal with the foreseeable risk of the large gaps in the railings that were of a size capable of allowing a child to slip through.

It was reported that the provider knew of this risk but continued to allow the fire escape to be used by children to enter and to leave the nursery. The defendant's lawyer disputed this in court and stated that the provider believed (wrongly) that the fire escape was safe as the nursery had been subject to a fire inspection and an inspection by Ofsted (www.telegraph.co.uk/Education/Educationnews/9562575/Nursery-fined-over-cover-upafter-fall-left-child-in-a-coma.html).

Legislation breached

A breach of duty under Section 3(1) Health and Safety at Work Etc. Act 1974:
'It shall be the duty of every employer to conduct his undertaking in such a way as to ensure, so far as is reasonably practicable, that persons not in his employment who may be affected thereby are not thereby exposed to risks to their health or safety.'[1] This is an offence under Section 33(1) (a) of the Act. The defendant also admitted to failing to notify the accident to the enforcement authority within the required time period as required under the RIDDOR 1995. These regulations have since been repealed and replaced by RIDDOR 2013.

Comments

Barry Berlin, prosecuting, said 'what we have here is a cover up of how the incident occurred and that is an obstruction of the authorities' (Berlin, B. www.telegraph.co.uk).

In passing his judgement, recorder Malcom Morse pointed out that Mr Ahmed had 'created a fiction' about the fall and 'it was, in a hackneyed but accurate phrase, an accident waiting to happen. The fact that it has not happened before, is, in my judgement, pure luck' (Morse, M. www.telegraph.co.uk). Eshan's mother, Sonia, said: 'You don't expect to see your child in that condition, especially when they are left at nursery. A place you trust to keep them safe' (Ahmed, S. www.telegraph.co.uk/Education/).

Falls from height

Reflection

- What checks do you make to ensure that your premises are safe for your staff and the children in your care?

- What procedures do you have in place for the reporting of defects?

- How do you make sure that repairs are completed and defects are dealt with?

Key point

It is an offence under the Health and Safety at Work Etc. Act 1974 to obstruct an Enforcement Officer.

The realisation of the seriousness of a situation can influence our decision-making processes. Professional honesty and integrity is crucial, always. It is never acceptable to fabricate evidence or be economical with the truth. Covering up and obstruction, as identified by the prosecutor in this case, brings into question the honesty and integrity of this particular owner and demonstrates a complete disregard for the welfare of the child in his care. Obstructing an Enforcement Officer is a separate offence under the Health and Safety at Work Etc. Act 1974 and is triable in the Magistrate's Court. There is currently a maximum penalty of £5,000.00

 Back to the team

Do staff feel confident to challenge unsafe actions by management?

 For the agenda

Is your setting a place that parents can trust to keep their children safe?

Remember, paperwork alone will not prevent accidents. It takes a combination of:

Key points ⚬━

- It is also important to consider the comment made by the defendant's lawyer that the defendant (wrongly) thought that the fire escape was safe to use because the nursery had been subject to both a fire inspection and an Ofsted inspection. A separate Act of Parliament and specific regulations cover health and safety matters. The enforcement of health and safety law in a child care setting is carried out either by authorised officers from the HSE or the local authority (usually the local council), depending on the nature of the business. Neither Fire Officers nor Early Years Inspectors are authorised to enforce health and safety requirements under the Health and Safety at Work Etc. Act 1974.

- Relying on the inspection of another enforcement body or indeed an inspection by the correct enforcement body does not fulfil the legal duty placed on the duty holder under health and safety law. It remains the employer's responsibility to identify the real health and safety risks associated with their business and to put steps in place to deal with those risks.
- The defence in any legal proceedings such as this case is that the defendant met their responsibility 'in so far as is reasonably practicable'. In this case, the risk of injury posed from the use of the fire escape was serious. It was foreseeable that a child could fall through the gaps and it was likely to happen, due to the use of the fire escape by children. Therefore, it was reasonable to expect steps to be taken to deal with this risk.
- The cost, time and inconvenience of providing guarding to the fire escape was low and grossly disproportionate to the high risk of an accident occurring and the severe consequences of any injury.

Case File 2: Logan Busby, aged 7 months

Date and nature of injury: 13 September 2011, head injury and concussion after falling off a metre-high nappy changing unit
Location: Lilliput Lodge Nursery, Hull
Magistrate's Court verdict: The defendant pleaded guilty.
Enforcement outcome: £3,000 fine, costs of £1,000 and a £15 victim surcharge
The nursery is no longer owned by Lilliput Lodge Limited.
(Source: www.hullcc.gov.uk/portal/page?_pageid=221,674011&_dad=portal&_schema=PORTAL&p_id=4847 , article entitled 'Company prosecuted for health and safety failure', by Hull City Council press release. Published: 21/10/2013 © Copyright of Hull City Council).

Background details

Logan attended Lilliput Lodge Nursery in Hull. He was being looked after in the baby room by a childcare assistant who was working alone with two other children. The nappy changing area was adjacent to the baby room and meant that children were unsupervised when nappy changing was required. The childcare assistant took Logan to have his nappy changed, but became distracted as she heard someone entering the baby room. In that moment of distraction, Logan fell off the changing unit, banging his head on the hard, concrete floor.

Contributing factors with links to the EYFS

- **Deployment of staff:** The childcare assistant was alone in the baby room. With three babies in her charge, the location of the changing area meant that she had to leave children unattended for nappy changing. Having staff working in baby rooms alone brings into question their capacity to meet every child's individual needs such as feeding or nappy changing and makes them vulnerable in the event of an emergency. The EYFS framework 3.28 outlines that 'staffing arrangements must meet the needs of all children and ensure their safety. Providers must ensure that children are adequately supervised and decide how to deploy staff to ensure children's needs are met' (DfE, Statutory Framework for the EYFS, 2014, p21).

- **Training:** The childcare assistant in charge of the children had not received sufficient training in the nappy changing procedures for the nursery. The EYFS framework 3.31 outlines that at least one person caring for children under two must be qualified to level 2. It also highlights the need for staff to have received training in order to meet the individual needs of children under two years old.

- **Risk assessment:** The investigation into this accident revealed that the risk assessment for the nappy changing activity was insufficient. The changing unit was a metre high. Therefore, the risk of babies falling or rolling off from this height was significant. The EYFS framework 3.64 outlines that staff need to be able to demonstrate how they are managing risks.

- **Health and safety records:** The nursery did not have records outlining what health and safety training staff had completed prior to the accident. The EYFS framework 3.20 outlines the requirements regarding staff qualifications, training, support and skills, which encompasses induction. All new staff must undergo induction training that includes guidance on relevant policies and procedures, including health and safety. Ongoing training opportunities for all staff indicates a genuine commitment to continuous improvement in ensuring children's safety and well-being.

- **Leadership and management:** The investigation revealed shortfalls in the manager's experience regarding health and safety. The EYFS framework 3.23 outlines the requirements expected for a manager and includes having a level 3 qualification and at least two years' relevant experience.

Contributing factors with links to the CCR/VCR

CR 1.8 Welfare of the children being cared for
CR 4.3 Qualifications and training (CCR Only)
CR 5.5 Suitability and safety of premises and equipment

Contributing factors under Health and Safety

- The childcare assistant was distracted and turned away from the child. The child then fell from the nappy changing unit onto the hard floor surface below.

A lack of an effective health and safety management system:

- A failure to assess the risk sufficiently and to implement control measures to reduce the risk of injury to children having their nappy changed. This was a foreseeable risk. The unit was a metre high and therefore the chance of young babies falling or rolling off the unit was significant.

- A failure to train staff in health and safety matters. This included the site manager, who had a responsibility for managing health and safety on site on a day-to-day basis.

- A failure to deploy suitable resources in terms of staff numbers to allow adequate supervision.

Legislation breached

Breach of duty under Section 3(1) Health and Safety at Work Etc. Act 1974:
'It shall be the duty of every employer to conduct his undertaking in such a way as to ensure, so far as is reasonably practicable, that persons not in his employment who may be affected thereby are not thereby exposed to risks to their health or safety.'[2]

This is an offence under Section 33(1) (a) of the Act. Breach of duty under Regulation 3(1) (b) of the Management of Health and Safety at Work Regulations 1999:
'Every employer shall make a suitable and sufficient assessment of . . .
(a) the risks to the health and safety of his employees to which they are exposed while they are at work: and
(b) the risks to the health and safety of persons not in his employment arising out of or in connection with the conduct by him of his undertaking, . . . for the purpose of identifying the measures he needs to take to comply with the requirements and prohibitions imposed upon him by or under the relevant statutory provisions. . . .'[3]
This is an offence under Section 33(1) (c) of the main Act.

---

[2]Page [82] extract from [Health and Safety at Work Etc. Act 1974] © Crown Copyright – Use subject to Open Government Licence v3.0 [http://www.nationalarchives.gov.uk/doc/open-government-licence/version/3/] – Except where otherwise stated.

[3]Pages [82] extract from [The Management of Health and Safety at Work Regulations 1999] © Crown Copyright – Use subject to Open Government Licence v3.0 [http://www.nationalarchives.gov.uk/doc/open-government-licence/version/3/] – Except where otherwise stated.

Councillor's comments

Councillor John Hewitt outlined the council's commitment to health and safety by saying, 'In cases where the consequences of an accident are potentially so severe or the safety controls are so inadequate, the Council will take formal action for the health and safety of the public'(Hewitt, J. www.hullcc.gov.uk/portal/page?_pageid=221,674011&_dad=portal&_schema=PORTAL&p_id=4847).

Key point

- Training your staff is an investment for your business. It is also a legal requirement.

Reflection

(STOP)

- What health and safety training do you provide new staff with before they start work?
- Think about the accidents you have had in your setting and the safety controls you have in place. Are you satisfied that the accidents could not have been prevented?

- How do you evaluate the impact that training has had?
- Is *everyone* in your setting committed to health and safety?
- What systems do you have in place to evaluate people's commitment to health and safety?

(ACTION)

- Keep a record of all health and safety training. It will help you to plan and assess training needs.
- Evaluate staff commitment using the diagram below:

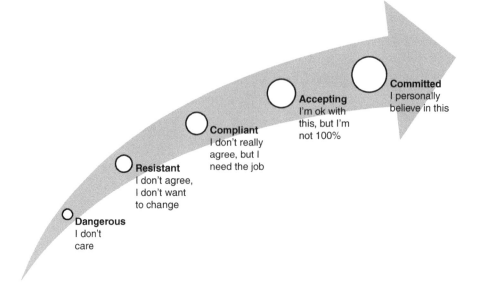

Dangerous
I don't
care

Resistant
I don't agree,
I don't want
to change

Compliant
I don't really
agree, but I
need the job

Accepting
I'm ok with
this, but I'm
not 100%

Committed
I personally
believe in this

Key point

It is worth considering the impact accidents and injuries can have on children and their families. It touches so many lives, just like a ripple effect on water.

Back to the team

Think about the most serious accident that has taken place in your setting:

Who was affected?

What control measures did you put in place?

Could it happen again?

Could it have been prevented?

For the agenda

Other areas to consider where falls from height have occurred and have resulted in injury include:

- play equipment
- stairways, e.g. stairs but also access to restricted areas such as to cellar areas
- windows.

Have you considered these areas in your risk assessments?

Reasons to inform and train and where to go for help

There are many reasons to train staff. The first is that an employer has a legal duty to do so and must provide staff with information so that they know how to do their job safely and without risks to their health. The second reason is to promote a positive safety culture within the business, where staff look out for each other, are actively involved in health and safety, and safe working is the accepted norm and practice. The Health and Safety at Work Etc. Act 1974 is very specific in what an employer is required to provide to support employees in their jobs. It requires the employer to provide 'such information, instruction, training and supervision as is necessary to ensure, so far as is reasonably practicable, the health and safety at work of his employees' (Section 2(2) (c)).

The Management of Health and Safety at Work Regulations 1999 are even more specific and tell an employer what information and training should be provided and when. This includes:

- when people start work (induction training)
- on exposure to new or increased risks (such as new equipment or changes in the workplace)
- on a change of job or responsibility
- also periodically to keep knowledge up to date (refresher training).

It is important to remember that there are many different types of training and it does not necessarily always require attendance or completion of a formal certificated course. For training to be effective it needs to be planned by identifying the training needs of the business and the people within it. Any training should also be reviewed to see if it has been effective. Have you ever evaluated health and safety training in your setting by looking to see if your staff are implementing what they have learned in practice?

The HSE has produced a guide to health and safety training. It takes an employer through the steps that they need to take, as well as suggesting different types of training methods. The guide, entitled 'Health and Safety Training: A Brief Guide', can be downloaded from the HSE website at: www.hse.gov.uk.

Key point ⚯

- Remember that young workers and those new to the workplace may be particularly at risk from accidents and will require extra training and a higher degree of supervision. There is currently no legal requirement under health and safety law to keep records of any health and safety training given to staff but it makes sense to do so. In an accident/incident situation it is very difficult to prove that you as an employer have fulfilled your legal obligations without a training record.
- Records also help you to plan training by identifying gaps and helping you to plan a training matrix or programme.

 Back to the team

Audit your setting:

Plan	
	Identify and prioritise what needs to be done through risk assessment.
	Deploy staff effectively to ensure that all children continue to be well cared for and supervised throughout the day.
	Identify the training needs of your organisation and make arrangements to implement your training plan.
Do	
	Discuss with staff their training needs and support them in improving their health and safety knowledge.
Check	
	Ensure that all staff understand procedures for specific care routines such as nappy changing.
	Check regularly for hazards within the environment, including equipment used to support children's care such as nappy changing units, babies' high chairs, and fire escapes.
	Make sure that staff have up-to-date health and safety training. Do not rely on training provided by past employers.

	Monitor the effectiveness of training. What improvements are visible as a consequence of training?
Act	
	Review and evaluate accidents.
	Always review any relevant risk assessment after an accident or a near miss.
	If you have not completed a risk assessment, then complete one as part of your investigation. It will help you to identify any gaps in your procedures.

Safety campaigns

Here are some examples of groups which actively campaign for child safety and have advice on children falling.

- www.rospa.com
- www.capt.org.uk
- www.patientsafetyfirst.nhs.uk

We also remember

The following children died as a result of playground falls.

Name and age	Year of accident	Nature of death	More information
Kian Williams, aged 3 years	2004	Playground accident: Kian banged his head on a flight of steps, causing bleeding on the brain and died five weeks later.	www.dailymail.co.uk, article entitled 'Headmaster blamed for death of pupil in playground fall wins appeal against conviction' by Luke Salkeld for the Daily Mail. © Associated Newspapers Ltd, the Daily Mail, The Mail on Sunday & Metro Media Group
Samuel Orola, aged 5 years	2011	Playground accident. Samuel had a heart attack on a school climbing frame and died.	www.dailymail.co.uk, article entitled 'Five-year-old boy "attempting trick" on nursery school climbing frame dies after falling and suffering heart attack' by Jamie McGinnes. © Copyright of Associated Newspapers Ltd, the Daily Mail, The Mail on Sunday & Metro Media Group

The following children aged under five also suffered as a result of falls.

Name and age	Year of accident	Nature of injury	More information
James Pitcher, aged 9 months	2004	Fall from height: James fell from a changing table, and sustained brain injuries. He is now quadriplegic.	www.news.bbc.co.uk, article entitled 'Large pay-out for brain injury boy' by Story from BBC NEWS © BBC
Billy Coniff, aged 2 years	2013	Fall from height: Billy fell out of a second floor nursery window and escaped serious injury.	www.birminghammail.co.uk, article entitled 'Angry mum calls for nursery to close after son's 20ft plunge' by Alison Stacey. © Birmingham Mail; Trinity Mirror Midlands
Michaela Eaton, aged 3 years	2013	Fall: Michaela cracked her head on the nursery railings while playing a game and suffered a deep cut above her eye.	www.birminghammail.co.uk, article entitled 'Three-year-old girl nearly blinded in fall at Birmingham nursery'. By Catherine Lillington. © Birmingham Mail; Trinity Mirror Midlands

8 Drowning

Chapter overview

Definition of drowning

Drowning: 'Die through submersion in and inhalation of water' (Oxford English Dictionary). According to CAPT, 'Babies and toddlers drown silently and can drown in as little as 5cm of water. So even rainwater collecting in a bucket can be a danger for a small child' (www.capt.org.uk). Children can drown at the beach, in holiday pools, swimming pools, garden ponds, lakes, quarries or in the bath. Public Health England (PHE) has recently issued guidance on the dangers of accidental child drowning involving the use of bath seats.

Statistics

According to the WHO, drowning is one of the ten 'leading causes of death for children and young people in every region of the world' (www.who.int). RoSPA collaborate with other organisations, including Water Incident Database (WAID), to collect and analyse drowning statistics as part of their injury data and surveillance. The average drowning statistics based on data from RoSPA between 2000 and 2013 is 404 a year (www.rospa. com). CAPT also collates data on drowning and, according to its statistics, in 2010 '28 children under 15 drowned in the UK. Three of these children were under one, 12 were between one and four, four were between five and nine, and nine were between ten and 14' (www.capt.org.uk). Thankfully, at the time of writing, there has not been a case of drowning in a day care setting since 2002.

Case File 1: Abigail Rae, aged 2 years

Date and nature of death: 28 November 2002, drowned in a pond

Location: Near to Ready Teddy Go Nursery, Lower Brailes, Shipston-on-Stour

Inquest verdict: Accident resulting from neglect

Enforcement outcome: A Crown Prosecution Service (CPS) spokesman said: 'After careful consideration by two senior CPS lawyers, two independent counsel, two expert witnesses and in consultation with the HSE it was decided that there was insufficient evidence to prosecute for gross negligence or health and safety offences.' The nursery never re-opened after Abigail's death.

(Source: www.news.bbc.co.uk/, article entitled 'Neglect ruling in girl pond death', by BBC News © BBC News)

Background details

Abigail went missing from the nursery and was found an hour later face down in a neighbouring pond, by her mother. Abigail was taken to Birmingham Children's Hospital, where she was pronounced dead on arrival.

Contributing factors with links to the EYFS

- **Supervision of children:** Abigail had only started at the nursery ten days prior to her death. Therefore, she would have been inquisitive to explore her new surroundings and not familiar with the daily routines. Abigail left the nursery unnoticed by any staff, through a gate that everyone presumed was closed. The EYFS framework 3.28 outlines the need for appropriate staffing ratios to be in place to ensure children are within sight and hearing of staff.

- **Safety checks not undertaken:** Staff assumed gates and doors were all locked. Had someone checked that the back gate was indeed locked, Abigail would not have been able to leave the nursery grounds and her death may have been prevented.

- **Lack of risk assessment:** Staff had not anticipated the hazards posed within their neighbouring area or anticipated the curiosity of a new child at the setting. The EYFS framework 3.64 outlines that 'Staff must be able to demonstrate how they are managing risks' (DfE, Statutory Framework for the EYFS, 2014, p28).

Contributing factors with links to the CCR/VCR

CR 5.1 Suitability and safety of premises and equipment
CR 5.2 Suitability and safety of premises and equipment (CCR Only)
CR 5.5 Suitability and safety of premises and equipment

Contributing factors under Health and Safety

It is not possible to comment in this section, as the CPS made a decision that there was insufficient evidence to prosecute.

Solicitor's comments

Rebecca Hearsey, solicitor for the Rae family, identified that Abigail's death was due to 'a failure of systems throughout the nursery with practices and procedures' (Hearsey, R. www.news.bbc.co.uk/go/pr/fr/-/1/hi/england/coventry_warwickshire/4837614.stm). This reinforces the importance of the need for staff practice to match paperwork. We must never presume all children will know and comply with safety rules.

Reflection

This case highlights the risk of drowning, particularly within the local neighbourhood. Supervision of children is so crucial, as is security of the setting.

- Consider the security of your setting and hazards within your locality.

- Think about how secure your setting is at different times of the day, after different activities. Could a child leave unnoticed?

- Think about your procedures regarding new children starting. Are staff alert to new children's curiosity?

- Review and evaluate the risk assessments with regard to security and locality hazards.

- Make safety checks a part of regular daily practice.

- Ensure new children are adequately supervised, especially during their first days at your setting.

- Discuss vigilance as part of professional supervision.

Key point ⚷

Children are unique, unpredictable individuals. There is no substitute for vigilance and being professionally curious.

Back to the team

Do staff **CARE** about vigilance? Do they:

- **C**heck
- **A**sk
- **R**eview
- **E**valuate

 Back to the team

Audit your setting:

Plan	
	Identify and prioritise what needs to be done through risk assessment.
Do	
	Discuss with staff the need to double check vulnerable areas within your setting.
	Review and evaluate induction procedures for new children.
Check	
	Make sure that all staff take on the responsibility to check locks, gates, doors etc.
Act	
	Learn from accidents, near misses, mistakes and experience, including those from similar businesses within your sector.

Safety campaigns

- www.riss.org.uk/water-safety/drowningpreventionweek.org.uk
- www.capt.org.uk
- www.gov.uk

9 Burns and scalds

> ## Chapter overview
>
> ### Definition of burns and scalds
>
> Burns are injury to tissue caused by heat, friction, electricity, radiation or chemicals. The severity of the injury depends on the degree of the burn and how seriously the tissue has been damaged. Scalds are a type of burn caused by hot liquids or steam.

Statistics

Recent figures from the Office for National Statistics (ONS) covering the period from 2008 to 2013 highlight the scale of the problem nationally regarding burns and scalds for children aged under five. The table below outlines the number relating to hospital admissions/ Emergency Department visits and deaths.

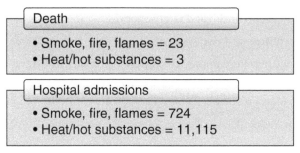

Death
• Smoke, fire, flames = 23
• Heat/hot substances = 3

Hospital admissions
• Smoke, fire, flames = 724
• Heat/hot substances = 11,115

(Source: 'Reducing unintentional injuries in and around the home among children under five years', Public Health England, 2014)

Burns tend to fall into three categories:

- superficial
- partial thickness
- full thickness.

Superficial burns usually damage the out layer of skin only, for example mild sunburn. Partial thickness burns usually require medical treatment as more layers of skin are damaged, resulting in painful blister. Full thickness burns are very serious and always require hospitalisation. All layers of the skin are damaged and nerve endings can be destroyed. Treatment usually involves skin graft and victims can be left with disfiguring scarring.

Key points ➔O

- Children are particularly vulnerable to burns and scalds as their skin is thinner than an adult's. Therefore, they can suffer a serious burn much more quickly. CAPT has conducted some research into the financial cost of in-patient treatment for a child, the total cost being £74,495. This figure gives an indication of the level of follow-up treatment required for these sorts of accidents (www.makingthelink.net).

- A momentary lapse of supervision can result in a burn or scalding accident that could mean long-term, painful follow-up treatment for the child.

Case File 1: Mya Hunt, aged 5 months

Date and nature of injury: 22 September 2005, second-degree burns to ear, neck and back

Location: Munchkins Nursery in Shard End, Birmingham

Birmingham Magistrate's Court verdict: The nursery owner, Suzanne Holmes, pleaded guilty to two health and safety offences.

Enforcement outcome: A two-year conditional discharge and costs of £4,795

(Source: www.birminghammail.co.uk/news/local-news/nursery-guiltover-tots-scalding-41331, article entitled 'Nursery guilt over tot's scalding', by Birmingham Mail. Published: 28 May 2007, 08:31, GMT © Birmingham Mail; Trinity Mirror Midlands).

Background details

Mya was strapped into a high chair for mealtime when a jug of hot custard spilled over her. The jug had been placed on a tray on a window sill and was accidently knocked off by a nursery nurse who had got up to attend to another child. Mya received second-degree burns to her ear, neck and back.

Contributing factors with links to the EYFS

- **Lack of risk assessment:** Magistrates in this case were of the opinion that this accident could have been avoided if proper risk assessments had been undertaken and implemented. The EYFS framework 3.64 states that 'Risk assessments should identify aspects of the environment that need to be checked on a regular basis, when and by whom those aspects will be checked, and how the risk will be removed or minimised' (DfE, Statutory Framework for the EYFS, 2014, p28).

- **Complacency regarding unsafe practices:** The window sill had been used to store various items on for at least two years prior to the accident. Placing children underneath the window sill increased the risk that any items which inadvertently fell off the window would hurt or injure a child. These unsafe behaviours, of using the window sill for storage and placing babies in high chairs underneath them, had become habits as they were left unchecked and unchallenged. Continual improvement of staff is crucial in ensuring they keep up to date with developments and helps to bring fresh impetus and perspectives and to tackle complacency in a setting. The EYFS framework 3.20 states: 'Providers must support staff to undertake appropriate training and professional development opportunities to ensure they offer quality learning and development experiences for children that continually improves' (DfE, Statutory Framework for the EYFS, 2014, p2).

Contributing factors with links to the CCR/VCR

CR 5.1 Suitability and safety of premises and equipment
CR 5.5 Suitability and safety of premises and equipment

Contributing factors under Health and Safety

- The unsuitable use of the window sill as a shelf. In this case a jug of hot custard was placed on the sill.

Failure to implement an effective health and safety management system:

- A failure to carry out a suitable and sufficient risk assessment and a failure to identify the risk of placing items on the window sill with a child in the vicinity.

- A failure to identify and eliminate an unsafe practice that had become custom and practice over time.

The practice of using the window sill as a shelf had continued for some time before this accident took place. It had gone unchallenged. (Source: www.birminghammail.co.uk/news/local-news/nursery-guilt-over-totsscalding-41331).

Key point 🔑

- Just because something has become an accepted custom and practice does not make it safe. Challenge unsafe actions.

Legislation breached

Breach of duty under Section 3(1) Health and Safety at Work Etc. Act 1974:

'It shall be the duty of every employer to conduct his undertaking in such a way as to ensure, so far as is reasonably practicable, that persons not in his employment who may be affected thereby are not thereby exposed to risks to their health or safety.'[1] This is an offence under Section 33(1) (a) of the Act. Breach of duty under Regulation 3(1) (b) of the Management of Health and Safety at Work Regulations 1999:

'Every employer shall make a suitable and sufficient assessment of:

(a) the risks to the health and safety of his employees to which they are exposed while they are at work: and

(b) the risks to the health and safety of persons not in his employment arising out of or in connection with the conduct by him of his undertaking,

for the purpose of identifying the measures he needs to take to comply with the requirements and prohibitions imposed upon him by or under the relevant statutory provisions. . .'[2]

This is an offence under Section 33(1) (c) of the main Act.

Magistrates' comments

'When parents entrust young children to the professional care of others, it is then the duty of those others to ensure those children are safe at all times' (Birmingham Magistrates. www.birminghammail.co.uk).

Reflection

These types of injuries can be disfiguring for children and require lengthy hospital treatment. Also consider other heat sources in the environment that could cause accidents, such as radiators, hot pipes, hot surfaces and hot water.

- Have you considered sources of heat in your risk assessments?

- Have you also considered the way children will behave?

- Do you carry out workplace health and safety audits?

---

[1]Page [96] extract from [Health and Safety at Work Etc. Act 1974] © Crown Copyright – Use subject to Open Government Licence v3.0 [http://www.nationalarchives.gov.uk/doc/open-government-licence/version/3/] – Except where otherwise stated.

[2]Page [96] extract from [The Management of Health and Safety at Work Regulations 1999] © Crown Copyright – Use subject to Open Government Licence v3.0 [http://www.nationalarchives.gov.uk/doc/open-government-licence/version/3/] – Except where otherwise stated.

Back to the team

It is important to ensure that the environment is suitably furnished and safe for children at all times. Furniture and storage should be looked at with a critical eye to identify potential hazards. For example:

- Could a bookcase be pulled over by a child?
- Can children reach things on shelves?
- Are children's tables, chairs and cots placed underneath shelves or window ledges? Does this pose a hazard?

Key point ⚍O

- It is never acceptable to ignore unsafe behaviours or conditions. If you do, you are partially responsible for any subsequent accidents.

Lessons learned for the future

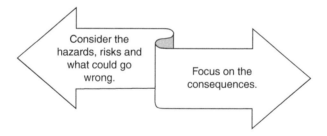

Consider the hazards, risks and what could go wrong.

Focus on the consequences.

Active systems of monitoring such as workplace audits can help to identify unsafe or unsuitable practices. These audits can be completed by staff, provided that they are confident and know what to do, that the findings are supported by management and that they are actioned. It is good practice to involve a number of different staff on a rotational basis. Alternatively, members of staff could audit each other's areas.

Back to the team

Audit your setting:

Plan		
		Identify and prioritise what needs to be done through risk assessment.
		Plan the work environment and try to eliminate hazards through design.
Do		
		Encourage all staff to look at the environment with a critical eye.
		Encourage and support staff to challenge unsafe actions or behaviours.
Check		
		Make sure that all staff understand the developmental needs of the age range of the children they are caring for and can plan activities and the environment accordingly.
		Carry out peer safety inspections/audits of different rooms to help identify risks and hazards and avoid complacency.
Act		
		Prioritise health and safety and ensure staff can access specialist training.

Safety campaigns

- www.cbtrust.org.uk/
- www.capt.org.uk
- www.nhs.uk
- www.childsafetyeurope.org
- www.makingthelink.net

We also remember

The following children also suffered injuries due to burns and scalds.

Name and age	Year of accident	Nature of injury	More information
Casey White 17 months old.	2008	Casey suffered burns to the face, neck, chest and stomach after entering the kitchen and pulling a cup of scalding water on herself.	www.news.bbc.co.uk, article entitled 'Ofsted probes scalding at nursery'. By Story from BBC NEWS © BBC
Harrison Farrell, aged 5 years	2012	Harrison suffered second-degree burn to his thigh after staff spilt hot chicken fat on his leg.	www.dailymail.co.uk, article entitled 'Mother sues nursery after staff spilt burning CHICKEN FAT on her five-year-old son leaving him with second degree burns'. By Harriet Arkell © Associated Newspapers Ltd, the Daily Mail, The Mail on Sunday & Metro Media Group
Freya Brooker, aged 15 months	2014	Freya suffered third-degree burns to her fingers. The nursery claimed she had sustained injuries by sucking her fingers but eventually, after Social Services became involved, the nursery admitted that Freya had burned her hand in its care.	www.dailymail.co.uk, article entitled 'Doctors threatened parents with having their 15-month-old daughter taken away because they could not explain burns – which she suffered at NURSERY'. © Associated Newspapers Ltd, the Daily Mail, The Mail on Sunday & Metro Media Group

10 Infectious diseases

Definition of infectious diseases and foodborne illnesses

'Infectious diseases are caused by pathogenic microorganisms, such as bacteria, viruses, parasites or fungi; the diseases can be spread, directly or indirectly, from one person to another. Zoonotic diseases are infectious diseases of animals that can cause disease when transmitted to humans' (www.who.int).

'Foodborne diseases encompass a wide spectrum of illnesses and are a growing public health problem worldwide. They are the result of ingestion of foodstuffs contaminated with microorganisms or chemicals. The contamination of food may occur at any stage in the process from food production to consumption ("farm to fork") and can result from environmental contamination, including pollution of water, soil or air' (WHO http://www.who.int). Food poisoning is 'any disease of an infectious or toxic nature caused by or thought to be caused by the consumption of food or water' (Food Safety Act 1990, as amended).

Statistics

Our research has shown that mainly three infectious diseases have affected day care settings and been reported in the press. These are:

- salmonella
- E. coli
- tuberculosis (TB).

The chart below shows that incidents of E. coli have been the most prevalent in day care settings. For links to the press articles, see the Useful links section at the end of the book.

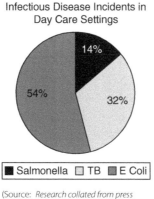

Infectious Disease Incidents in
Day Care Settings

14%

54%

32%

■ Salmonella □ TB ■ E Coli

(Source: *Research collated from press articles, 2000–15*)

Date and nature of incident: A total of 139 children under five years old and eight adults were diagnosed with *Salmonella enteritidis* phage type (PT) 12.

Location: The source of the outbreak was attributed to Cannock House Day Nursery.

Crown Court verdict: Cannock House Day Nursery Ltd pleaded guilty.

Enforcement outcome: Fined £40,000 (£20,000 per offence) plus £2,920.73 costs, with the judge saying larger fines would have been awarded if funds had been available. Full costs would also have been awarded if funds were available. The nursery is now run by a different company.
((Source: www.newsshopper.co.uk/news/4402651.CHELSFIELD_40_000_fine_after_nursery_salmonella_outbreak/, article entitled 'CHELSFIELD: £40,000 fine after nursery salmonella outbreak', by Court Reporter. Published: Thursday 28 May 2009 © Copyright of Newshopper; Newsquest (London) Ltd)).

Background details

Over the weekend of 17/18 March 2007, three children attended a hospital Emergency Department with bloody diarrhoea. After tests over the next few days a total of 139 children under five years old and eight adults were diagnosed with *Salmonella enteritidis* PT 12. The source of the outbreak was attributed to Cannock House Day Nursery. Once investigations started into the suspected salmonella cases, various professionals including Environmental Health expressed concerns that hygiene conditions and practices at the nursery were poor. Salmonella was found on one child's face flannel, two chopping boards and three mixing bowls. Ofsted suspended the nursery's registration for six weeks.

Contributing factors with links to the EYFS

- **Poor hygiene practices:** Investigations revealed that there were inadequate supplies of cleaning/hygiene materials such as soap, paper towels and toilet rolls. Lack of access to these essential items means good hygiene routines are compromised. In addition, children's face cloths were not changed on a daily basis and were reused for more than a week. This, coupled with poor nappy changing and potty training procedures, significantly increased the risk of cross-infection. The EYFS framework 3.60 states that 'providers must ensure there are suitable hygienic changing facilities for changing any children who are in nappies and providers should ensure that an adequate supply of clean bedding, towels, spare clothes and any other necessary items is always available' (DfE, Statutory Framework for the EYFS, 2014, p28).

- **Unhygienic food preparation and kitchen appliances in poor condition:** The kitchen contained appliances and equipment suitable for domestic use only. Considering the nursery catered for 136 children and 50 staff this was deemed to be inappropriate. In addition to meals being provided by the nursery, the children participated in cooking activities. Salmonella was later found on chopping boards, mixing bowls and face flannels. The EYFS framework 3.48 states that food preparation needs to be done hygienically and by competent, trained people.

- **Premises in an unclean and poor state of repair:** A lack of investment in the premises and equipment and a failure to implement recommendations from previous inspections meant that the nursery providers compromised children's safety and well-being. The EYFS framework 3.54 states that the premises must be fit for purpose. It also states: 'Providers must comply with requirements of health and safety legislation (including fire safety and hygiene requirements)' (DfE, Statutory Framework for the EYFS, 2014, p27).

- **Poor infection control systems:** There were no systems in place to minimise the spread of cross-infection when cleaning, such as colour-coded cloths. A lack of sluice facilities meant that children's soiled potties, clothing and nappies could not be cleaned adequately. The nursery did not have a robust policy or procedure regarding the exclusion of children who are ill or infectious. The judge included comments about the setting's failure to control the outbreak in his summing up. The EYFS framework 3.44 states that 'a provider must promote the good health of children attending the setting. They must have a procedure, discussed with parents and/or carers, for responding to children who are ill or infectious, take necessary steps to prevent the spread of infection, and take appropriate action if children are ill' (DfE, Statutory Framework for the EYFS, 2014, p25).

- **Poor staff training with regard to policies and procedures:** Training is crucial to ensure staff understand their roles, responsibilities and provider's expectation with regard to ensuring children safety and welfare. All new staff must undertake induction training as outlined in the EYFS framework 3.20. In addition, it is expected that staff preparing/handling food have received food hygiene training as outlined under the EYFS framework 3.48.

Contributing factors with links to the CCR/VCR

CR 1.8 Welfare of the children being cared for
CR 5.1 Suitability and safety of premises and equipment

Contributing factors under Health and Safety

This was a very complex and detailed investigation. At the time *Salmonella enteritidis* PT 12 was associated mainly with eggs and poultry. These bacteria were isolated from faecal samples taken from those affected and on a face flannel and on chopping boards. Classroom cooking did take place and included the use of raw shell eggs. Salmonella can spread through cross-contamination from raw food such as eggs to other foods, food contact surfaces or food equipment. It can also spread from person to person by poor hygiene, such as failing to wash hands thoroughly after using the toilet.

In this case, a number of issues arose:

- Failure to heed warnings of previous inspections.
- Failure to implement a food safety management system based on HACCP (Hazard Analysis Critical Control Point). This is a legal requirement under food safety law.
- Failure to implement a proper cleaning regime, including deep or steam cleaning surfaces such as carpets. Proper environmental cleaning is essential in outbreak control.
- Failure to equip the kitchen properly.
- Failure to keep the nursery environment in a good state of repair.
- Failure to ensure adequate supplies of hygiene equipment.
- Failure to train staff properly.
- Failure to implement a proper system to exclude children.

These are all management issues that should have been addressed. During the investigation, the Enforcement Officer served a number of enforcement notices to secure improvement. (Source: www.cieh.org/uploadedFiles/Core/Membership/Regional_network/London/News_and_Events/Perspectives-Case-Study.pdf).

Key point ➴

- Teach children how to wash their hands properly and why it is important. This is a valuable life skill, like learning to cross the road.

Legislation breached

Breach of duty under Section 2(1) Health and Safety at Work Etc. Act 1974. The Act places a general duty on an employer to ensure, so far is reasonably practicable, the health, safety and welfare of their employees at work.

Breach of duty under Section 3(1) Health and Safety at Work Etc. Act 1974:

'It shall be the duty of every employer to conduct his undertaking in such a way as to ensure, so far as is reasonably practicable, that persons not in his employment who may be affected thereby are not thereby exposed to risks to their health or safety.'[1]

Both are offences under Section 33(1) (a) of the Act.

Judge's comments

Judge Heather Baucher said,

'We could have been dealing with a number of fatalities here. I do consider this to be a grievous breach. I can see for myself that the premises were in a state.'

(Baucher. H. www.newsshopper.co.uk/news/4402651.CHELSFIELD_40_000_fine_after_ nursery_salmonella_outbreak/).

Key point

- Food poisoning is particularly serious for certain groups of people such as the young, the elderly, those already ill or with a suppressed immune system and those with food allergies.

 Back to the team

Think about how food is prepared in your setting and how hygiene overall is managed. Are you satisfied all staff follow guidelines regarding good hygiene practice? Act on and action any points from your food safety inspections by the Enforcement Officer. If you are unsure about the advice or disagree with the advice given, then discuss the matter with the inspecting officer or their manager. Ignoring the advice is likely to lead to future problems. Both you and the Enforcement Officer share the same goals – the production of safe food and keeping the children in your care safe and healthy.

Reflection

- The scale and spread of this outbreak is a pertinent reminder of how serious food poisoning can be. This is reiterated by the judge's comments in this case (see above).

- Do you have a robust infection control policy in place?

THINK

- Do staff know what to do if an outbreak of gastroenteritis occurs?

- How do you know that your infection control policy works and is being followed?

For the agenda

Have you ever used a desktop case study to train staff on what to do if an outbreak occurs? Enforcement Officers train like this!

 Back to the team

What do you teach children about food hygiene and keeping food safe during interactive cooking activities?

Where to go for help and advice

Public Health England has produced guidance on infection control entitled 'Guidance on infection control in schools and other child care settings'. This can be downloaded from the Government website at www.gov.uk

Many local authorities have produced their own guidelines on infection control, which may be available on their websites. If you suspect that there is an outbreak at or connected to your setting, then you should notify your local Food Safety Enforcement Officer and the Infection Control Nurse in your local Health Protection Team.

Key points ⚬O

- Have you got a plan for dealing with outbreaks of food poisoning and gastroenteritis?
- Do your infection control procedures deal effectively with the risk from environmental contamination of soft furnishings, carpets, toys?

A word about your food handlers

Regulation EC No. 852/2004 Chapter II Article 4(2) Annex II Chapter VIII Requirement 2

The law requires that food handlers must tell their employer if they are suffering from any illness or condition that may affect food safety. This is because they can contaminate food and make it unsafe to eat if they are suffering from certain conditions such as:

- diarrhoea and/or vomiting
- discharge from the gums, mouth, ears or nose
- sore throat with fever

- a recurring bowel problem
- a recurring skin ailment
- any other ailment that could affect food safety
- any cuts or sores open or that are infected.

Key points ➖O

- If food handlers are ill and have certain infections then they can pass this on to others by contaminating food, food contact surfaces and work equipment. Based on guidance from Public Health England, any food handler suffering from diarrhoea and/or vomiting should be excluded from the premises for a period of 48 hours *after their symptoms have ceased*. If they have been taking anti-diarrheal medication they must still wait 48 hours to be symptom-free after taking the medication. This is because even when symptoms have stopped the person can still be infectious and transfer food poisoning bacteria and viruses by poor personal hygiene.
- Do your food handlers follow the 48-hour rule? In certain circumstances providers may need to consider asking for medical clearance via the General Practitioner (GP) through the submission of faecal specimens, before allowing a food handler to return to work. This may be based on the type or the persistence of the symptoms or subsequent diagnosis of an illness, for example E. coli 0157 or an illness such as gastroenteritis following holiday travel.
- You need to apply the same rules to your other staff and children, as cases of gastroenteritis, food poisoning and foodborne illness will spread rapidly throughout a setting.
- You can obtain advice from your Food Safety Enforcement Officer/Environmental Health Officer on dealing with isolated cases of food poisoning, foodborne illness or other infectious diseases.
- Providers must have a strict policy on staff illness and their staff must be aware of this policy and follow it.

Even though this incident does not relate to a specific day care setting, we felt it was important to include it, as many nurseries and playgroups organise visits to farms. This type of outing promotes many of the learning and development outcomes. It is a good opportunity to help promote children's physical development, particularly with regard to teaching children about the importance of good hygiene practice and hand washing. This is a worthwhile and exciting learning opportunity that we would positively encourage, providing organisers know the risks and minimise the hazards accordingly.

Date and nature of injury: August/September 2009, more than 90 children affected by the E. coli 0157 bacteria after visiting the petting zoo and stroking animals

Location: Godstone Farm, East Surrey

London's High Court (civil claim) verdict: The civil claims were settled with substantial damages being paid.

((Source: www.gov.uk/government/uploads/system/uploads/attachment_data/file/342361/Review_of_major_outbreak_of_E_coll_o157_in_surrey_2009.pdf)).

Background details

Following a visit to Godstone Farm, over 90 children contracted E. coli 0157. This particular strain of E. coli can make children critically ill and cause haemolytic uraemic syndrome (HUS) and acute renal failure. During the visit, the children did wash their hands thoroughly and used anti-bacterial gel. However, the Griffin Report into this outbreak concluded that hand washing alone is insufficient to prevent an outbreak that is caused through contact with animals and their faeces. Some of the children have been left with kidney damage, high blood pressure and other health complications.

Contributing factors with links to the EYFS

- **Safeguarding and welfare requirements:** The overall requirement of the EYFS framework 3.2 is about ensuring that providers do all they can to ensure that children are kept safe and well, including promoting children's good health. It is crucial if planning this type of trip that organisers have considered the potential health risks posed by farms and petting zoos and can demonstrate how these risks have been minimised and/or removed.

- **Outings:** The EYFS framework states that children must be kept safe on outings. It outlines the need for a risk assessment to cover the outing, but states that this does not always need to be in wiring. However, in this instance, it would be useful to outline to parents though a letter, with a copy of the risk assessment, the risks associated with visiting farms and the ways in which the staff will protect the children in their care. The EYFS framework 3.65 covers outings.

- **Risk assessment and safety checks:** The purpose of a risk assessment is to demonstrate how risks are being managed and how children will be kept safe. A risk assessment is not a substitute for common sense, professionalism or supervision. The EYFS framework 3.64 covers risk assessment and refers to the HSE guidance available on risk assessment.

Contributing factors with links to the CCR/VCR

CR 1.1 Welfare of the children being cared for

Contributing factors under Health and Safety

E. coli 0157 is often carried in the gut of animals, especially ruminants – cattle, sheep and goats – and it is often present in their faeces. It has also been detected in their saliva. Infection may arise from contaminated food and water or through direct or indirect contact with animals, their faeces and their environment. As with all food poisoning and foodborne illness, young children and the elderly are particularly vulnerable. This type of infection is also virulent, as not many bacteria are required to make a person ill. It has what is known as a 'low infective dose'. It can spread rapidly from person to person via the faecal–oral route. Scrupulous hand washing is an important control in preventing and limiting spread.

E. coli 0157 is one of a number of VTEC E. coli. These bacteria produce a toxin or poison, and bloody diarrhoea is often a symptom. Infection can also cause serious conditions affecting the blood, the kidneys and the central nervous system. Compared to other types of food poisoning, cases of E. coli 0157 are low. However, as can be seen from this outbreak, the consequences are severe and the impact is high because of the way the bacteria are spread and the effect that they can have on the body. This was a major outbreak and the investigation and report produced by Professor Griffin made recommendations for the farm owners and also the regulatory bodies such as the NHS (clinical services), the HPA, local authorities and the HSE.

The report made many detailed recommendations including:

- the need to introduce measures to reduce the risk of contact with faecal matter by layout and design of public areas in open farms
- the need to increase awareness of the risks of animal contact among farm owners, regulatory authorities and visitors
- an approved code of practice to be developed for open farms in consultation with the industry
- the need for prompt identification and control of outbreaks and better interagency working
- research to assist clinicians in the rapid diagnosis of E. coli 0157
- research aimed at preventing or limiting the carriage of the bacteria by animals.
  (Source: www.gov.uk/government/uploads/system/uploads/attachment_data/file/342361/ Review_of_major_outbreak_of_E_coll_o157_in_surrey_2009.pdf)).

Infectious diseases

Solicitor's comments

Solicitor Jill Greenfield said: 'I can see that a day out to a farm is for many seen as a chance to get back to nature, from the rigours of the city and for children to meet and touch animals. How tragic that these young children were allowed to skip into this farm completely oblivious to the danger that awaited' (Greenfield, J. (www.getsurrey.co.uk/news/surrey-news/godstone-farm-ecoli-outbreak---7059615).

Reflection

- Consider your policies and procedures for conducting outings with children.

- Think about hand washing arrangements for outings. Do you rely on alcohol gel? This needs to be in addition to hand washing, and not a substitute.

- Review and evaluate your policies and procedures for conducting outings.
- Ensure the importance of hand washing is included in your planning prior to a visit taking place.

Key point ⚊O

It is worth remembering that one of the complications of VTEC E.coli such as 0157 is haemolytic uraemic syndrome (HUS), which is a notifiable disease. Here is the link for more information on notifiable diseases: https://www.gov.uk.

Where to go for help and guidance

After the outbreak at Godstone Farm an inquiry led by Professor Griffin published a report, which can be found here:

- www.gov.uk

Following the recommendations of the Griffin Report, the HSE reviewed their guidance AIS23 on 'Preventing or controlling ill health from animal contact at visitor attractions'. This guidance has now been withdrawn and the information has been replaced by an industry code of practice. This is available at the following link: www.visitmyfarm.org. There is information both for those planning visits, such as teachers, and for farm owners providing public attractions. The code of practice makes it clear that there needs to be a site-specific risk assessment carried out by the operator of the attraction and gives detailed guidance on how this should be completed and what should be included.

The website allows you access to download the code of practice and there is also a step-by-step guide to planning a farm visit. The emphasis is on good preparation, including a pre-outing visit to familiarise yourself with the facilities and the controls. Ask for an information pack, a copy of the site-specific risk assessment and the public liability insurance certificate.

Another useful source of information is: www.foodsafety.gov

Key points ⚬━O

- E. coli 0157 is a life threatening risk and the only way to eliminate this completely is to avoid contact with animals and their faeces. You, the parents/carers and the children need to know about this risk and it is the parents' or carers' choice as to whether their child is allowed to pet and feed the animals.
- It is also important that hand washing is supervised on such visits to ensure that it is thorough. This will be your responsibility. You can teach children the importance of this and demonstrate thorough hand washing techniques as preparation for the visit. This also needs to be reinforced during the visit. The code of practice contains lots of useful pictures that can be used. The HSE has also produced a video on the risk of E. coli 0157 and the importance of hand washing on its website at: http://www.hse.gov.uk. Although this section has highlighted the dangers of E.coli 0157, there are other infections that can be acquired through animal contact.
- Teach children about risk. This is how they learn.

Back to the team

Audit your setting:

Plan	
	Identify and prioritise what needs to be done through risk assessment.
	Update and renovate premises and equipment to ensure these are fit for purpose.
	Have your food safety management system in place.
	Have an outbreak plan in place.
	Identify and communicate key responsibilities.
	Plan outings such as those to open farms.
	Communicate the risks to parents and carers to allow informed decisions to be made.
Do	
	Discuss with staff expectations about hygiene practices and ensure these are followed consistently.
	Train your staff and tell them about your outbreak plan.
	Allocate clear responsibilities among staff.
Check	
	Ensure that all staff have up-to-date food hygiene training, especially if they are preparing/handling food.
	Carry out your own internal audits and checks to make sure procedures and policies are understood and being followed.
	Investigate any food complaints, suspected food poisonings and outbreaks. Review your policies to establish what went well and what could have gone better.
	Take action to address any issues or gaps.
	Ensure that site-specific risk assessments and public liability insurance for visitor attractions are in place.
Act	
	Minimise any outbreaks by ensuring exclusion procedures are clearly understood by all staff and implemented consistently.
	Notify any outbreak or suspected outbreak to the food safety Enforcement Officer.
	Communicate with parents and carers during an outbreak. It is important that they understand the risks. They are likely to support you and co-operate if they are kept informed about the situation.
	In an outbreak situation, collect and collate as much information as you can about the cases, e.g. onset time, duration, symptoms, food histories.

Safety campaigns

Every year the FSA and the local authorities run a Food Safety Week to promote a topical problem. In May 2015 it was the Chicken Challenge aimed at reducing the incidence of campylobacter food poisoning by half.

- www.hse.gov.uk
- www.who.int
- www.food.gov.uk
- www.food.gov.uk

We also remember

The following cases have been reported in the press and are all related to tuberculosis (TB):

Year of incident	More information
May 2001	www.telegraph.co.uk, article entitled 'Three children at nursery have TB'. By Celia Hall, Medical Editor © of Telegraph Media Group Limited
January 2003	www.news.bbc.co.uk, article entitled 'TB alert at nursery school'. © BBC
October 2008	www.mirror.co.uk, article entitled 'Nursery hit by TB scare'. © The Daily Mirror, published by MGN Ltd, part of Trinity Mirror plc
March 2009	www.news.bbc.co.uk, article entitled 'Nursery children screened for TB'. © BBC
September 2011	www.heraldscotland.com, article entitled 'Children to be screened as nursery worker catches TB'. By Alison Campsie © Herald & Times Group
April 2014	www.scotsman.com, article entitled 'Motherwell nursery worker tests positive for TB'. © The Scotsman
May 2015	www.theargus.co.uk, article entitled 'Parents in uproar about delay in warning of TB-infected person at nursery'. © The Argus; Newsquest Media (Southern) Ltd

For more information on TB, see the links here:

- www.nurseryworld.co.uk
- www.nice.org.uk
- www.gov.uk

11 Incidents/Near misses

Definition of incidents/near misses

Incident: An unplanned event or occurrence that affects or has the potential to affect the health, safety or security of:

- people
- assets.

Case File 1: Boy, aged 2 years

Near miss: Incident that has not resulted in any injury or damage but had the potential.

Date and nature of injury: November 2012, leg fracture while playing on a trampoline intended for use by older children

Location: Caring Daycare, Haslemere

Guildford Magistrate's Court verdict: Caring Daycare pleaded guilty.

Enforcement outcome: The nursery was fined £7,500 plus £5,250 in prosecution costs and victim surcharges.
(Source: www.getsurrey.co.uk/news/nursery-fined-after-two-year-old-boy-6520361, article entitled 'Nursery fined after two-year-old boy on trampoline broke leg', by Jennifer Morris: 17 January 2014, 17:50 GMT © Copyright of Get Surrey; Surrey Advertiser Group).

Background details

A two-year old boy was playing on a trampoline, supervised by staff. However, according to the manufacturer's instructions and guidance the trampoline was intended for home use only and by children aged six years and over. A risk assessment had been carried out for the activity, but was completed by an untrained member of staff.

Contributing factors with links to the EYFS

Equipment not suitable for the age of the child: This nursery was clearly trying to plan and implement challenging and enjoyable activities in addition to focusing on the prime areas of learning for its youngest children. However, the use of a trampoline that was not intended to be used by children under six years old compromised the safety of the activity, resulting in the accident. The Statutory Framework for the EYFS 3.54 outlines the need for providers to ensure that their premises and activities provided overall are safe and suitable for the age range of the children being cared for.

Risk assessment completed, but by an untrained member of staff: It is imperative that staff know and understand how to complete a risk assessment. This includes being able to identify hazards and risks and identifying how these will be made safe or what control measures need to be in place. The Statutory Framework for the EYFS 3.64 outlines guidance on risk assessment, with a footnote to refer to the HSE for more detailed guidance on risk assessment.

Contributing factors with links to the CCR/VCR

CR 1.8 Welfare of the children being cared for
CR 5.1 Suitability and safety of premises and equipment
CR 5.5 Suitability and safety of premises and equipment

Contributing factors under Health and Safety

- The equipment was not suitable for the age of the child using it.

- There was a failure to follow the manufacturer's instructions about the use of the equipment.

- The person undertaking the risk assessment was not trained and may not have had the background, knowledge and experience to be deemed competent to complete this task.

- There was a failure to adequately assess the suitability of the equipment in the circumstances in which it was being used.

Legislation breached

Breach of duty in Section 3(1) of the Health and Safety at Work Etc. Act 1974:
'It shall be the duty of every employer to conduct his undertaking in such a way as to ensure, so far as is reasonably practicable, that persons not in his employment who may be affected thereby are not thereby exposed to risks to their health or safety.'[1] This is an offence under Section 33(1) (a) of the Act.

Comments

Nursery owner Peter Churchley said: 'The accident happened because a well-intentioned initiative to help children learn to balance and exercise safely was inadequately implemented. This resulted in an unfortunate accident which will never happen again at the nursery as we removed the trampoline immediately afterwards' (Churchley, P. www.getsurrey.co.uk/news/nursery-fined-after-two-year-old-boy-6520361). Waverley Borough Councillor, Donal O'Neill, said: 'This case highlights the importance of following health and safety guidelines. Often they are quoted as spoiling people's fun, but in this instance what should have been an enjoyable day at nursery resulted in a serious injury for a little boy because the guidance was not followed' (O'Neill, D. www.getsurrey.co.uk/news/nursery-fined-after-two-year-old-boy-6520361).

---

[1] Page [116] extract from [Health and Safety at Work Etc. Act 1974] © Crown Copyright – Use subject to Open Government Licence v3.0 [http://www.nationalarchives.gov.uk/doc/open-government-licence/version/3/] – Except where otherwise stated.

Reflection

This case encapsulates the dichotomy faced by providers in striving to achieve outstanding learning and development opportunities, while ensuring that children are safeguarded. This particular activity was focused on physical development, a prime area of learning. The Statutory Framework for the EYFS 1.5 states, 'Physical development involves providing opportunities for young children to be active and interactive; and to develop their co-ordination, control, and movement' (DfE, Statutory Framework for the EYFS, 2014, p8). Trampolines have become very popular and are viewed as an enjoyable way to exercise. However, it is crucial that guidelines are followed.

- Think about the toys and equipment in your setting. Do you follow manufacturers' instructions when using play equipment?

- Is the equipment suitable for the age/stage of development of the child/children using it?

- Has a risk assessment been completed prior to use?
- Was the person completing the assessment competent?

Key point ⚊O

It is worth remembering that supervision of children alone, is not sufficient in itself to prevent accidents and that other things too, need to be present as highlighted in this case.

Risk assessments

There is a myth that risk assessments have to be complicated and complex in detail. This can often mean that providers and staff may not feel confident and are anxious about 'missing something'. It can also sometimes lead to a focus on imaginary or trivial risks in a well-intended effort to cover every conceivable scenario. This is not necessary. The degree of complexity required in a risk assessment depends on the nature of the business and the risks within it.

Risk assessment is the identification of the hazards in your business. It examines the likelihood of harm occurring and the consequences. It considers:

- what could happen

- who might get hurt

- how severe the impact or consequences will be

- how likely it is that something will happen.

It looks at the existing control measures or safety precautions in the business. It tells you if you are doing enough or what else you need to do to protect your employees and other people. In any risk assessment it is important to concentrate on real, actual risks and not on trivial or insignificant risks. An example of an 'insignificant health and safety risk' is demonstrated in the HSE's advice provided by its 'Myth Buster's Panel' in response to a query about a school banning children from playing conkers, unless they were wearing safety goggles. HSE advised that the health and safety risk to children playing with the conkers was insignificant/trivial and that any children deliberately hitting each other over the head with conkers was a discipline issue and not a health and safety issue. (www.hse.gov.uk/myth/september.htm) For medium and small businesses HSE's advice is to keep it simple. A good start is to walk around your workplace and identify the hazards within it and those that arise from the work that is done there. There are five steps in the risk assessment process. These are detailed in the diagram below.

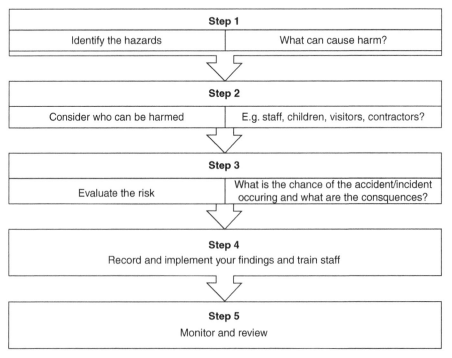

| **Step 1** | |
| Identify the hazards | What can cause harm? |

| **Step 2** | |
| Consider who can be harmed | E.g. staff, children, visitors, contractors? |

| **Step 3** | |
| Evaluate the risk | What is the chance of the accident/incident occuring and what are the consquences? |

| **Step 4** |
| Record and implement your findings and train staff |

| **Step 5** |
| Monitor and review |

(Source: *Five steps to risk assessment based on the HSE's guidance*)

Where to go for help and advice

Guidance on how to carry out risk assessments is available on the HSE website:

* www.hse.gov.uk

You do not need a formal qualification to carry out a risk assessment but the Management of Health and Safety at Work Regulations 1999 require that an employer appoint a 'competent' person to assist in health and safety matters such as risk assessment. Consider whether you or someone inside your business has the skills to carry out the risk assessments. Information is available from a variety of sources, such as trade associations or the HSE website (see above). If you do not have the skills then you may need to get help from a competent source outside of the business. Even if you employ a consultant to help you, remember no one knows your business as well as you and your staff do. So you and they need to be involved with the risk assessments.

 Back to the team

Audit your setting for risk from equipment:

Plan	
	Identify and prioritise what needs to be done through risk assessment.
Do	
	Plan activities that are suitable for the age and stage of the children's development, paying particular attention to the resources to be used.

Check		
	Do all staff know what to look for when completing risk assessments?	
	Are your staff competent and confident to undertake risk assessments if they are required to complete them?	
Act		
	Challenge unsafe practices/behaviours.	
	Remove and/or restrict the use of toys and equipment for children in line with manufacturers' guidance and instructions.	
	Warn parents and/or carers of the dangers of children using toys and/or equipment that is not appropriate for the children's age or stage of development.	

Case File 2: Asbestos exposure incident

Date and nature of incident: 11 January 2012, asbestos released in an uncontrolled manner

Location: Little Smarties Nursery, Cheltenham

Cheltenham Magistrate's Court verdict: Both the nursery owners and the contractor pleaded guilty.

Enforcement outcome: The nursery owners, Gerard and Gisela Gray, were fined £6,000 plus £1,000 in costs. The contractor, Pzemyslaw Sikora, was fined £500 plus £250 in costs.

(Source: www.punchline-gloucester.com/articles/december2014/cheltenham childrens nursery prosecuted after asbestos exposure, article entitled 'Cheltenham children's nursery prosecuted after asbestos exposure', by Punchline, December 2012 © Copyright of Moose Partnership Ltd).

(Source: www.cheltenham.gov.uk/news/article/1166/a_cheltenham_business_and_contractor_prosecuted_after_asbestos_Exposure , article entitled 'A Cheltenham business and contractor prosecuted after asbestos exposure', by Cheltenham Borough Council, Published Tuesday 2 July 13 © Cheltenham Borough Council).

Background details

The nursery owners appointed a contractor to carry out some painting work in the porch area of the nursery. As the porch was in a poor state of repair it was decided to demolish it instead. However, the porch contained asbestos insulating board and the contractor failed to undertake an asbestos survey prior to the demolition of the porch. The owners should not have authorised any demolition work to be undertaken without first ensuring asbestos was not present. In the event, asbestos was released in an uncontrolled manner, thereby exposing individuals in the vicinity to risk of contamination from asbestos.

Contributing factors with links to the EYFS

- **Safety and suitability of premises and environment:** While the providers were well intentioned in trying to ensure their premises were being maintained in a suitable condition, failure to undertake the proper surveys prior to commencing work meant that they had committed an offence. The EYFS framework 3.54 emphasises the need for providers to 'comply with requirements of health and safety legislation (including fire safety and hygiene requirements)'. There is further guidance on working with asbestos at www.hse.gov.uk/asbestos.

Contributing factors with links to the CCR/VCR

CR 5.1 Suitability and safety of premises and equipment

Contributing factors under Health and Safety

- A failure by the contractor to implement a safe working method for the demolition of the porch that resulted in the uncontrolled release of asbestos fibres.
- A failure by the provider and the contractor to recognise or assume the presence of asbestos containing materials (ACMs).
- A failure by the provider to undertake a suitable and sufficient risk assessment prior to the work commencing and to communicate this.
- A failure by the provider to control the work undertaken by the contractor. Also a failure to ensure that the contractor followed a safe work method to implement control measures to reduce the release of asbestos fibres.

Certain types of work to encapsulate, seal or remove ACMs need to be carried out by a licensed contractor under strict conditions. This is dependent on the risk of fibre release from the work. Again, detailed guidance is given on the HSE website.

Legislation breached

Providers: Breach of duty under Section 2(1) of the Health and Safety at Work Etc. Act 1974. This places a general duty on an employer to ensure, so far is reasonably practicable, the health safety and welfare of his employees at work. This is an offence under Section 33(1) (a) of the Act.

Breach of Regulation 5 of the Control of Asbestos at Work Regulations 2006, Identification of the presence of asbestos:

5. 'An employer shall not undertake work in demolition, maintenance, or any other work which exposes or is liable to expose his employees to asbestos in respect of any premises unless either . . .

(a) he has carried out a suitable and sufficient assessment as to whether asbestos, what type of asbestos, contained in what material and in what condition is present or is liable to be present in those premises;

or . . .

(b) if there is doubt as to whether asbestos is present in those premises he—

(i) assumes that asbestos is present, and that it is not chrysotile (white asbestos) alone, and

(ii) observes the applicable provisions of these Regulations.'[2]

In April 2012 new regulations were introduced that consolidated existing asbestos laws and the management of ACMs in non-domestic premises. The law requires the 'duty holder' to manage asbestos in premises. This is an offence under Section 33(1) (c) of the main Act. The contractor was prosecuted for a breach of Section 3 of the Health and Safety at Work Etc. Act 1974.

Reflection

This case is a reminder about accountability and legal responsibility, as both the nursery owners and the contractor were fined. Any employer engaging a contractor to work on the premises will have a duty to ensure that the health and safety of the contractor and anyone else who is affected by their actions is protected. This will include your staff, children and any visitors to the premises. The contractor will also have health and safety responsibilities.

(STOP)

- Think about how renovation/maintenance work is organised in your setting. Are you satisfied that all risks are minimised?
- Have you identified the source and condition of any ACMs on your premises?

(THINK)

- Have you shared this information with your maintenance contractor or maintenance staff?

(ACTION)

- Have you formulated a plan to deal with the risks from ACMs that are or may be present?

 (margin text, rotated) Coping With Crisis

It is not good enough to allow the contractor to 'get on with the job', as is demonstrated in this case. A failure to manage how contractors work on premises can result in accidents and incidents. As in this example there are many cases where both the employer and the contractor have been prosecuted for health and safety breaches. You need to work closely with any contractor and ensure that they are familiar with your premises and your emergency procedures. For example, you would need to advise them if there are ACMs present and, if there are, what condition they are in and whether the proposed work will disturb them. You in turn need to understand what the contractor is doing and how they propose to do it. You both need to work together to identify risks and to put control measures in place to deal with significant risks.

Key point 🔑

Control contractors who carry out work on your premises.

Where to go for help and advice

Any building or house built or refurbished before the year 2000 may contain asbestos and/or ACMs. Examples of ACMs include asbestos cement sheet, asbestos insulation boards, asbestos lagging and textured decorative finishes such as Artex. Damaged or disturbed asbestos or ACMs can result in the release of asbestos fibres, which when inhaled can result in the development of asbestos related diseases. These diseases take a long time to develop but are very serious. Due to the delay in time between exposure, disease development and symptoms, by the time the disease is diagnosed, it is often too late to do anything. It is estimated that 20 tradespeople per week die as a result of asbestos related disease from past exposure. Very often they are exposed without knowing (www.beware-asbestos.info). For this reason the Control of Asbestos Regulations 2012 place a duty on people who manage non-domestic premises. You are a duty holder if:

- you own the building
- you are responsible through a tenancy agreement or contract
- you have control of the building but no tenancy agreement or contract
- in a multi-occupancy building, you are the owner and you have taken on responsibility for control of maintenance or repair.

A duty holder's responsibility is:

- to check to see if asbestos or ACMs are present or are likely to be present
- to check what condition the materials are in
- to assume that the material contains asbestos unless you are sure that it does not

- if planning maintenance or refurbishment of the building, to consider having a specialist sample the material. This also needs to be considered if the material is damaged
- to record the location and the condition of the material on a plan or drawing
- to decide if the condition or the location of the materials makes their disturbance likely
- to formulate and implement a plan to manage these risks.

Detailed guidance is available from the HSE website at http://www.hse.gov.uk/asbestos/. The HSE's guidance leaflet 'Managing Asbestos in Buildings: A Brief Guide' INDG 223 (Rev 5) 04/12 is also available at www.hse.gov.uk

This tells you what a duty holder must do. It includes advice on action to take depending on the condition of the ACMs. There is also information to help you to identify what types of building materials may contain asbestos.

Back to the team

Audit your setting for asbestos risks:

Plan		
	Identify and prioritise what needs to be done through risk assessment.	
	Prepare for any building work/renovations meticulously and ensure the correct surveys and permissions have been sought.	
Do		
	Identify and assess the presence of any ACMs on site and put a plan in place to manage risks from them.	
Check		
	Go over the risk assessments and work methods provided by your contractors (ask them for a copy).	
	Make sure that contractors are working to your site rules and their method statements.	
	Check that contractors working on premises/buildings are aware of their duties under health and safety.	
Act		
	Challenge unsafe practices/behaviours.	
	Stop unsafe work actions as soon as you see them.	

Safety campaigns

Beware asbestos. www.beware-asbestos.info

Date and nature of incident: 7 June 2006, children from Clockwork Day Nursery were taken on an outing to a local park. Sidney Holt, aged four years, slipped and fell 24 metres before being impaled on a tree branch.

Location: Stamford Park, Ashton-under-Lyne

Both Clockwork Day Nursery and Tameside Metropolitan Borough Council (MBC) were prosecuted.

Trafford Magistrate's Court verdict: Clockwork Day Nursery pleaded guilty. **Enforcement outcome.** The nursery were ordered to pay £21,000 fine and £6,799.10 costs. The nursery later appealed this fine and lost its case.

Manchester Crown Court verdict: Tameside MBC managed the park. The Council pleaded guilty for failing to ensure that children were protected from risks and failing to carry out a proper risk assessment of the water spillway before the accident.

Enforcement outcome. It was fined £25,000 and ordered to pay £23,565 costs.

Improvement notice: An Improvement Notice was served by the HSE on Tameside MBC after the accident. The notice required the erection of fencing of the water spillway to prevent access by children. This notice required the work to be completed within a specified period of time. The notice was complied with.

(Source: vscg.co.uk/case-law/stamford_park_hse_prosecution, article entitled 'Stamford Park – HSE prosecution', by Visitor Safety in the Countryside Group. Published 2009 © Copyright of Visitor Safety in the Countryside Group).

Background details

A group of 20 children aged between four and eleven years were taken on a trip to Stamford Park, Ashton-under-Lyne. Four members of staff accompanied the children, although one member of staff had not been cleared to supervise the children and the other was the nursery's handyman. The group also included a child who required one-to-one supervision. Despite this, the children were allowed to play unsupervised and out of sight/hearing of staff. Sidney Holt, aged four, was attempting to cross some water, when he slipped on some algae and was swept 24 metres to the bottom of a water spillway and became impaled on a branch at the end of the spillway, sustaining serious stomach injuries. Other children returned to the staff to inform them of the accident, but the staff did not believe the children. Sidney was found by a passer-by, who called an ambulance. It was only then, 15 minutes later, that staff realised what had happened and the severity of the accident. (Source: www.vscg.co.uk).

Contributing factors with links to the EYFS

- **Risk assessment:** It is clear that the pre-planning stage of this trip was inadequate as staff did not take reasonable steps to ensure that children were not exposed to risk as outlined in the EYFS framework 3.64. It is imperative with outings that practitioners are proactive about identifying potential trouble spots. Conducting a pre-visit, or asking establishments to send their own risk assessments prior to a visit taking place, gives an opportunity to appraise the risks in conjunction with the needs and age group of children taking part in the outing.

- **Staff:child ratios/supervision:** It is clear that this particular group were of a wide age range and some children required one-to-one attention. This should have been planned for prior to the outing. It is also concerning that staff were not aware when the accident had happened and a member of the public contacted the emergency services. It is imperative when planning outings that there are sufficient capable and qualified staff accompanying children. Staff need to be aware where children are at all times and certainly be within sight and hearing of children, as outlined in framework 3.28 of the EYFS.

- **Outings:** The EYFS framework 3.65 states that 'Children must be kept safe while on outings' (DfE, Statutory Framework for the EYFS, 2014, p29). Taking children to new places can be a stimulating and educational experience for them and is to be encouraged. However, as this case highlights, children need to be safe and, in the event of an emergency, staff need to be familiar with procedures for summoning help while ensuring all children in the group are safe.

Contributing factors with links to the CCR/VCR

CR 1.8 Welfare of the children being cared for
CR 5.5 Suitability and safety of premises and equipment

Contributing factors under Health and Safety

- Children, including the accident victim, were able to gain access to the water spillway. In attempting to cross the water, Sidney slipped on some algae and was swept to the bottom of the spillway.

- A failure by the provider to assess the surroundings and the activity of the outing.

- A failure by Tameside MBC to assess the risk posed to park users by the water spillway. This was particularly relevant in relation to children.

- A failure by the provider to provide adequate resources for the outing in terms of numbers of competent staff. There was a requirement to provide a suitable level of supervision to meet the needs of the group.

- A failure by Tameside MBC to recognise and take action to deal with a significant and foreseeable risk.

Legislation breached

The provider and Tameside MBC were prosecuted separately for two breaches of health and safety law. These were the same breaches.

Breach of duty under Section 3(1) Health and Safety at Work Etc. Act 1974:

'It shall be the duty of every employer to conduct his undertaking in such a way as to ensure, so far as is reasonably practicable, that persons not in his employment who may be affected thereby are not thereby exposed to risks to their health or safety.'[3] This is an offence under Section 33(1) (a) of the Act. Breach of duty under Regulation 3(1) of the Management of Health and Safety at Work Regulations 1999:

'Every employer shall make a suitable and sufficient assessment of . . .

(a) the risks to the health and safety of his employees to which they are exposed while they are at work; and

(b) the risks to the health and safety of persons not in his employment arising out of or in connection with the conduct by him of his undertaking,

. . . for the purpose of identifying the measures he needs to take to comply with the requirements and prohibitions imposed upon him by or under the relevant statutory provisions. . ..'[4]

This is an offence under Section 33(1) (c) of the main Act.

Reflection

Good planning and knowing the group of children well should ensure a safe and fun trip. This particular case highlights the weaknesses in both pre-planning and the lack of vigilance for this outing, as a consequence of which a child was injured. The HSE said, 'These cases are not about stopping children having fun. However, there is an obligation to protect vulnerable people from dangers. Supervision is critical and should reflect the needs of the party, the activities being carried out, the age and ability range of the children, and the risks of the location' (www.vscg.co.uk).

- Consider how trips and outings are planned for and organised in your setting.

- What are your emergency procedures while on an outing, such as who will call an ambulance, who is the qualified first aider?

- Review and evaluate procedures for trips and outings. Reflect on previous excursions, and make a note of what needs to be changed and/or done differently.

For the agenda

Have a full team discussion about the trips and outings, reflecting on this particular case.

Where to go for help and advice

The HSE has produced guidance for schools on organising school trips. This has come about as a number of health and safety myths have built up around this issue relating to what should and should not be done. This in turn has led to reluctance by schools and their teachers to become involved in school outings due to a fear of prosecution or civil action. Although aimed at schools, there are many useful links, case studies and a leaflet entitled 'Tackling the Myths' on the website that may be useful to providers.

The key message once again is not to manage risk through reams of paperwork but to focus on how you are going to manage the 'real' risks by taking sensible and proportionate steps that are relevant to the planned trip or activity. Good planning is essential and staff involved in planning need to be properly supported. You can access the case studies and frequently asked questions from the HSE webpage at: www.hse.gov.uk.

 Back to the team

Audit your setting for outings:

Plan	
	Identify and prioritise what needs to be done through risk assessment.
	Organise pre-visits for off-site activities, if possible, and ask venues for a copy of their risk assessment.
	How will you inform parents and/or carers about the trip?
Do	
	Discuss with staff their training needs and ensure they feel confident in managing the health and safety of the trip, especially if they will be caring for children with specific needs such as allergies or asthma. How will they handle an asthma attack or a wasp/bee sting while on an outing?
	Make sure that sufficient staff accompany the children to meet their individual needs and ensure children are adequately supervised.
Check	
	Do all staff know what to look for when completing risk assessments for outings?
	Do staff understand expectations around supervision while on outings?
Act	
	Take everything needed to keep children safe on outings, such as first aid box, asthma inhalers, and EpiPens if required by particular children or staff.
	Review previous outings and update risk assessments accordingly. Share this information with all staff.

Case File 4: A toddler injured by defective play equipment

Date and nature of injury: August 2006. A toddler sustained serious laceration to the head that required surgery.

Location: Leap Frog Nursery, Northwich

Vale Royal Magistrate's Court verdict: Leapfrog Day Nurseries Ltd pleaded guilty to failing to ensure the health and safety of the child.

Enforcement outcome: £10,000 fine

(Source: www.hse.gov.uk/lau/pdfs/lauprosecutions0708.pdf, article entitled 'Health and safety offences and penalties in local authority enforced sectors 2007/2008', by Health and Safety Executive. Published 2008 © Copyright of Health and Safety Executive).

(Source: www.crewechronicle.co.uk/news/local-news/nursery-fined-10000-after-girl-5635077, article entitled 'Nursery is fined £10,000 after girl injured', by Crewe Chronicle. Published 23 May 2007 © Copyright of Crewe Chronicle).

Background details

A child at Leap Frog Nursery in Northwich sustained 'a serious laceration' to her head while playing on defective play equipment. The tricycle had rusty areas of exposed metal and was unsafe to be used by children.

Contributing factors with links to the EYFS

- **Safety of toys and equipment:** It is clear that this particular piece of equipment was not suitable to be used by children, yet no one had deemed it unsafe and thought to remove it. Continual use, especially of popular toys, will mean the toy/equipment may need replacing/replenishing sooner than anticipated, thus rendering a financial implication. However, keeping a piece of defective equipment and allowing children to continue to use it, is dangerous, irresponsible and a false economy as the above case, with a fine of £10,000, illustrates. The EYFS framework 3.54 covers safety and suitability of premises, environment and equipment.

- **Risk assessment and safety checks:** This piece of equipment should have been identified as faulty/defective and removed from use as part of the daily safety checks. Check what is included in your risk assessment with regard to toys, equipment and resources. The EYFS framework 3.64 covers risk assessment.

Contributing factors with links to the CCR/VCR

CR 1.1 Welfare of the children being cared for
CR 5.1 Suitability and safety of premises and equipment
CR 5.5 Suitability and safety of premises and equipment

 ## Back to the team

Sometimes checking the same things every day can lead to complacency. It is useful to have staff check areas they may not be as familiar with in order to identify different hazards.

Key point ⚷

Ensure that all staff know what to look for when undertaking safety checks. Talking to children about safety and involving them in the process of identifying potential hazards is both educational and can be illuminating.

Contributing factors under Health and Safety

- A defective piece of play equipment was available for use by children.

- The policy for the regular inspection of equipment was not implemented at this site at the time that the accident took place.

Key point ⚷

Procedures for inspecting equipment and dealing with defective equipment need to be implemented.

A lack of an effective health and safety management system:

- to ensure that defective equipment was taken out of use.

- to ensure that the procedure for the checking of equipment was being implemented effectively.

Key point ⚷

A defective piece of equipment increases the risk of an accident/injury.

Legislation breached

Section 3(1) of the Health and Safety at Work Etc. Act 1974:

'It shall be the duty of every employer to conduct his undertaking in such a way as to ensure, so far as is reasonably practicable, that persons not in his employment who may be affected thereby are not thereby exposed to risks to their health or safety.'[5]

The offence for failing to meet this duty is detailed in Section 33(1) (a) of the Act.

Reflection

Supervision of children needs to include how children are using equipment and, if new hazards emerge as children play, these can be addressed in order to prevent accidents. Public Health England (PHE) has identified the importance of training in relation to accident prevention and children under five years as a key action area for local authorities and their partners. 'The early years workforce needs support and training to enable it to strengthen its central role in helping to reduce unintentional injuries' (Public Health England, 'Reducing unintentional injuries in and around the home among children under five years', PDF, June 2014).

- What procedures do you have in place for dealing with defective equipment?

- Are staff aware of this procedure?

- How do you check that this procedure is being followed?

Key point

It is crucial that staff are safety aware at all times. Anticipating risks is much more proactive than crisis management.

Incidents/Near misses

Back to the team

Audit your setting for defective equipment:

Plan	
	Include toys, equipment and resources in the risk assessment.
Do	
	Have a system for staff to report faults/concerns about toys, resources and equipment.
Check	
	Make sure that staff undertake regular safety checks of toys, equipment and resources and ensure defective pieces are removed.
Act	
	Discuss safety regularly at staff meetings.

Case File 5: Food hygiene regulations breach

Date and nature of incident: July 2010 Sparklings Nursery was closed by Birmingham Environmental Health department after mouse droppings were repeatedly found in its kitchen. The nursery re-opened in September 2010.

Location: Sparkling's Day Nursery, part of the Ashiana Community Project, Sparkbrook, Birmingham

Birmingham Magistrate's Court verdict: Ashiana Community Project pleaded guilty to one count of breaching food hygiene regulations.

Enforcement outcome: The project was fined £2,500 and ordered to pay £1,475 in costs and a victim surcharge.
(Source: www.birminghammail.co.uk/news/local-news/fine-for-miceinfested-birmingham-nursery-161394, article entitled 'Fine for mice infested Birmingham nursery', by Paul Suart. Published 15 September 2011 10.30 GMT © Copyright of Birmingham Mail, Trinity Mirror Midlands).

Background details

Sparkling's Day Nursery, part of the Ashiana Community Project in Sparkbrook, Birmingham was prosecuted for food hygiene breaches. During four separate visits by environmental health officers, mouse excrement was evident on worktops, in sinks, behind fridges and throughout the food preparation area. Live mice were discovered behind the fridge. This, coupled with a strong smell of mouse urine, clearly indicated an infection and was a wholly unsuitable environment for preparing food for babies and children.

Contributing factors with links to the EYFS

- **Food and drink:** It is worrying to think that food was being prepared in this kitchen that was clearly unhygienic. There was evidence of an infestation on four separate visits by environmental health officers. Staff working in the kitchen on a daily basis must also have noticed the smell, mouse droppings or seen mice. Framework 3.48 of the EYFS states, 'There must be suitable facilities for the hygienic preparation of food for children'. It also states that 'all staff who are preparing and handling food must receive training in food hygiene' (DfE, Statutory Framework for the EYFS, 2014, p26).

- **Safety:** The Statutory Framework for the EYFS is clear in signposting providers' duties under health and safety. These include compliance with food hygiene regulation. Framework 3.54 states, 'providers must comply with requirements of health and safety legislation (including food safety and hygiene requirements)' (DfE, Statutory Framework for the EYFS, 2014, p27).

Contributing factors with links to the CCR/VCR

CR 1.1 Welfare of the children being cared for
CR 5.7 Suitability and safety of premises and equipment (CCR only)

Contributing factors under Food Safety

- A failure by management to act on advice of the pest control company and the local authority to deal with the problem of an infestation by mice

---

Key point 🔑

- The presence of rats and mice in food premises, where they pose an imminent risk of injury to health, will result in the closure of the food premises or the part of the premises affected.

Legislation breached

At the time that this prosecution took place, the requirements of Regulation EC 852/2004 on the hygiene of foodstuffs was enforced under the Food Hygiene (England) Regulations 2006. The EC regulation sets out the requirements that food business operators (FBOs) must comply with. This includes the general requirements that a food premises must comply with.

Annex II Chapter 1 states that food premises are to be kept clean and in good repair and condition and that the layout, design and construction should permit good food hygiene practices including protection against contamination and in particular pest control.

Magistrate's comments

Magistrate Alan Last said, 'Ashiana had adopted a casual and cavalier approach towards pest control. What concerns me was the length of time it took to get the organisation to provide a safe environment for [a] vulnerable group of people – young children' (Last, A. http://www.birminghammail.co.uk/news/local-news/fine-for-mice-infested-birmingham-nursery-161394).

Reflection

It is worth remembering that being in possession of a food hygiene certificate does not abolish the need for a clean and hygienic food preparation area.

- Have you checked for any signs of food pests?

- Have you actioned any recommendations or requirements from your Enforcement Officer or pest control contractor?

- How do you check that your premises are being kept clean and are free of pests?

 Back to the team

- Why is it important to keep food pests out of our premises?
- Audit your setting for pest infestations.

Pest control

Effective pest control is an essential part of any food safety management system as food pests carry bacteria, can contaminate food and make it unsafe to eat in a variety of ways. Rodents such as rats and mice in particular can contaminate food, food surfaces and preparation areas with their fur, droppings and urine. They will also contaminate food by trying to eat it. They will gnaw food packaging to get to the food source. They also can cause significant damage to property by gnawing through structure, electrical cables etc.

Rats and mice carry fleas, mites and ticks as well as bacteria and viruses that can kill. This includes salmonella, E. coli, listeria and cryptosporidium. Rat urine can cause a disease known as leptospirosis (also known as Weil's disease). The symptoms may cause a range of symptoms from mild flu to jaundice and kidney failure. In serious cases this disease can be fatal.

Key points ⚬O

- Babies and young children in particular are susceptible to food poisoning and foodborne illnesses as their immune system is still developing. They are seen as an at risk group.
- Rats and mice are considered to be such a serious risk to public health that in circumstances where they are present in a food business and there is an imminent risk, an Enforcement Officer may serve a notice to close the premises or to stop an activity immediately. This notice must be approved at the Magistrate's Court. As can be seen from the above case file, a prosecution is also a likely outcome.
- Pest control contractors, like any other contractor, need to be managed when they visit a site. It is important to monitor what they do and to action any recommendations. This may include taking steps to proof the building to prevent the pests gaining access. If a pest control treatment is being undertaken for rats or mice, it will only be successful if the premises are clean. Rats and mice will not take bait if there are other food sources available such as dirt and build-ups of food debris.
- If you are engaging the services of a pest control contractor, they should be competent. Ask to see copies of the training certificates for their staff. Ask for a copy of these records to keep on your file. Check to see if they are a member of a recognised professional trade association such as the British Pest Control Association (BCPA) or the National Pest Technicians Association (NPTA).

 Back to the team

Plan	
	Undertake regular inspections of food preparation area.
Do	
	Have a preventative approach to infestations.
	Act on advice and recommendations from your pest control contractor.
	Act on the requirements and recommendations made by your Enforcement Officer.

Check	
	Do staff know what to look for with regard to food pest infestations and problems?
	Do staff know that they must report any signs of pests immediately?
Act	
	Ensure that staff are aware of procedures to follow if they see any evidence of infestation.

Safety campaigns

The Foods Standards Agency (FSA) has a list of campaign information that you can access to promote good food hygiene in business and in the home. This information can be accessed at:

• www.food.gov.uk

There is also a variety of resources that can be downloaded from the website that can assist you in managing food safety. These are available at:

• www.food.gov.uk

We also remember

The following children also suffered injuries due to accidents:

Name and age	Year of accident	Nature of injury	More information
Brandon Dunseath, aged 5 years	2009	Eye injury: the child's eye was pierced by the handle of a 'table football' table.	www.bbc.co.uk, article entitled 'Ballymena nursery fined over child's eye injury'. © BBC News Northern Ireland
Mia Bush, aged 3 years	2011	She suffered a deep laceration to the little finger of her left hand, which cut an artery and sliced a nerve and tendon in her finger. The wound was 1cm wide.	www.southwalesargus.co.uk, article entitled 'Newport girl was injured with pair of scissors at nursery'. © South Wales Argus; Newsquest Media (Southern) Ltd

12 Key lessons

Chapter Overview

'Children are vulnerable. They look up to us, to look out for them. We aspire to give children a voice in an adult world' (www.childrens-charter.org).

Accidents are a part of everyday life. How preventable accidents are, is the subject of much debate. Accidents resulting in deaths are the subject of an inquest and Coroners have judged some of the tragedies and incidents in this book to be the result of a completely unforeseen accident. However, as our research has shown, recurrent themes underpin other tragedies and accidents outlined throughout this book. Where the accidents or incidents could have been prevented, there is a commonality of errors, oversights, lack of understanding/professionalism and apathy in each case.

Accident analysis

Having analysed all cases highlighted in this book, we can categorise issues into the following areas. Contributing factors to the accidents were:

- staff/unsafe behaviour
- ineffective risk assessment/safety checks
- ineffective arrangements for first aid
- defective equipment
- unsafe access/premises
- parents' advice/children's needs ignored
- poor food hygiene practice.

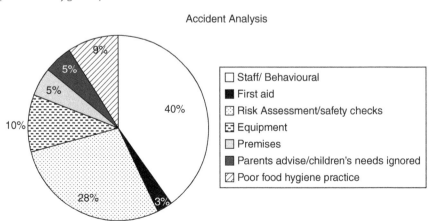

Accident Analysis

- ☐ Staff/ Behavioural
- ◼ First aid
- ▦ Risk Assessment/safety checks
- ⊡ Equipment
- ☐ Premises
- ◼ Parents advise/children's needs ignored
- ▨ Poor food hygiene practice

(Source: Based on analysis of cases covered in this book)

Staff behavioural issues and accidents

It is no surprise that the accident analysis illustrates that the main cause of these accidents and incidents was staff behaviour. How often have you heard or said that an accident or incident was down to human error? However, having come to that conclusion, what effort is then made to establish why the human failure occurred in the first place?
Was it due to:

- a lapse in concentration because the staff member was distracted, as in the Logan Busby case?
- a mistake through a lack of training or the adoption of bad custom and practice as the accepted norm, for example the use of the windowsill as a shelf on which to place a jug of hot custard in the case of Mya Hunt?
- a deliberate violation, such as ignoring the rules on the use of a mobile phone in the Rhiya Malin case?

So, if we conclude that human error is the main cause of an accident or incident, what were the reasons behind these behaviours and were these ever addressed as part of the investigation? Providers need to create a working environment where staff will admit if they have made a mistake or done something wrong. This will be dependent on how you carry out your accident/incident investigations and how you deal with blame. Staff should be in no doubt of what is acceptable and what is unacceptable behaviour in your setting. They should be encouraged and supported in challenging unsafe behaviour. They also need to be aware of the consequences of unsafe behaviour and how these matters will be dealt with.

The root causes of accidents or incidents at work can often be attributed to management failures, a lack of planning or organisational issues. If these are not identified and addressed then they will continue to cause problems, and further accidents and incidents are likely to occur.

Key points 🔑

- Investigate accidents, incidents and near misses thoroughly to determine the immediate, underlying and root causes.
- So look at your accident/near miss data and investigate thoroughly to see what is going wrong and, more importantly, why it is happening. This will give you a clear indication of where the risks are in your business and whether you have identified the real risks through your risk assessment. Have you taken human behaviour into account?
- Take action to try to prevent the accident or a similar incident from happening again. This is the main purpose of any investigation. It is also good for morale, as staff can see improvements taking place and action being taken to address concerns and health and safety issues.

The prime purpose of an investigation is to prevent the incident from happening again. In the event of a serious accident, both the enforcing authority and your insurer will be unimpressed if you have failed to investigate and deal with the matter. Likewise recurrent breaches where warnings have not been heeded are likely to result in enforcement action. This reiterates the importance of health and safety being a personal value that involves:

- working safely
- being responsible and accountable for actions
- caring for others' safety
- reporting all accidents and near misses
- speaking up if you see poor practice/unsafe behaviour
- being a good role model.

 Back to the team

- Do you know what you need to do if an accident takes place?
- Do you know who to report it to?
- Do you know where to record the information?
- Do you know what accidents require notification under RIDDOR?

Leadership styles

'You do not lead by hitting people over the head – that's assault, not leadership' (President Dwight D. Eisenhower). Organisations, their values and how they are managed have an influence on how staff will behave.

The HSE identifies the keys to successful health and safety management as:

- leadership and management
- a skilled well trained workforce
- an environment where people are trusted and involved in health and safety. (Source: www.hse.gov.uk)

You as a provider need to understand and prioritise the health and safety risks in the business and clearly set out what you want to achieve and how you will measure this. You cannot manage health and safety effectively if you do not know what the risks are in your business. The principle of 'Plan, Do, Check and Act' will help you to keep things simple and uncomplicated in identifying and managing these risks. Procedures and systems are not enough if you do not encourage your staff to work safely, so it is important that you deploy sufficient resources for health and safety. Think about how very different the outcome of the accident involving Sidney Hunt would have been if sufficient staff had been deployed on the outing to enable the children to be supervised properly.

Health and safety needs to be an integral and not a separate part of the business. It is not a bolt-on task that nobody wants to take responsibility for. You need to demonstrate your commitment to health and safety, so make sure you have it as a recurring agenda item at team meetings. Here you can discuss what went well and what went wrong. Leading by example is crucial in demonstrating to staff a commitment to safety. This helps to develop a safety culture within your setting that everyone can contribute to. This, coupled with robust management and accountability, is crucial in ensuring quality care for all children.

Key point

Encourage your team to develop thoughtful/mindful practice. In outstanding settings, one of the contributing elements inspectors evaluate when making judgements about the overall quality and standards of the early years provision is that 'the setting's practice consistently reflects the highest aspirations for all children's safety, well-being and learning' (Ofsted, Early years inspection handbook, No 102101 https://www.gov.uk).

Key elements in the overall quality and standards of the early years provision are:
- consistency
- high aspirations
- legal requirements being met.

Back to the team

The key elements in quality can only be achieved through a team effort. How are you evaluating:

- consistent practice throughout your setting, both indoors and outside
- staff aspirations for every child
- if legal requirements are being met, every day, by everyone?

In the cases highlighted in this book, the behavioural aspects with regard to the Statutory Framework for the EYFS are ultimately all failings under leadership and management and can be categorised into four main areas:

1. Staff unfamiliar with policies and procedures
2. Failure to comply with other legislation
3. Inadequate leadership and management decisions
4. Lack of professionalism

In the case of Molly Cunliffe, the policy of the nursery was to conduct sleep checks every ten minutes. This would be typical for most nurseries. However, where issues arise is in settings where practice does not match written policies and procedures. In Molly's case, she was left unattended for 20 minutes, by which time she was dead.

It is imperative that you ensure that everyone understands your expectations regarding practice matching policies and procedures.

Key points ⚬O

- Check that everyone understands the setting's policies and procedures. In the case of Eshan Ahmed, the manager failed to make the relevant notifications when the accident happened. The Statutory Framework for the EYFS is clear about the need for settings to comply with other legislation and failing to do so is an offence.
- Remember, the focus of your business may be childcare but the Statutory Framework for the EYFS is not the only legislation you must comply with.

Other cases have highlighted many examples of inadequate leadership and management decisions:

- Knowingly running the nursery with insufficient qualified staff for the number of children attending.

- Leaving unqualified staff and/or students in charge of babies or to run the nursery.
- Inappropriate deployment of staff and qualified first aiders.
- Appointing first aiders without valid first aid training.
- Blatant disregard for health and safety policies and procedures that compromises children's safety and well-being.

Eshan Ahmed's case also highlights how, in a quest to apportion blame, individuals will tell lies, fabricate evidence and scapegoat junior staff. The manager fabricated a story about how the accident occurred and wanted staff to collude with his version of events. This can never be acceptable practice.

Professional integrity has to be the bedrock of leadership and management. Leadership and management is a daily challenge. It is imperative to have a vision of quality that is shared by the team and will not be compromised.

In the words of John Ruskin: 'Quality is never an accident. It is always the result of intelligent effort' (Garvey, D. and Lancaster, A. *Leadership for Quality in Early Years and Playwork*, 2010, p127). What does it take to be an outstanding leader?

According to Ofsted you will need to be:

- inspirational
- focused on pursuing excellence
- uncompromising
- striving to improve/exceed achievement
- understanding safeguarding and welfare requirements
- monitoring and evaluating how requirements are met
- targeting professional development
- organising high quality supervision
- clear about the impact of staff practice on outcomes for children
- working in partnerships with parents/carers and other agencies.

For more information, here is the link for the Early years inspection handbook: www.gov.uk

Reflection

- What type of a leader are you? Do you empower your staff?

- What type of a leader do you work for? Do you feel empowered?
- What does being empowered mean to you in practice?

- To empower staff, they need to feel:
- nurtured
- encouraged
- coached
- mentored
- supported.

This will enable them to perform and behave professionally, even in the absence of management.

A lack of professionalism has been highlighted in many of the cases in this book. In the case of Rhiya Malin, staff admitted to behaving differently if management were not present, for example by ignoring the nursery policy about the use of mobile phones while caring for children. In order to adhere to child protection guidance, all settings now have a policy about mobile phones.

Key points ⚬—O

- It should not be the responsibility of management to have to 'police' staff about not using mobile phones while on duty. Staff need to take personal responsibility for their own professional conduct.
- Issues around staff complacency and inadequate supervision of children are themes in most of the cases we have highlighted. For Rhiya Malin to be able to wander into the playhouse and not be missed by anyone, that no one saw or heard her, despite there being four members of staff outside with the children, seems inconceivable. This reiterates the importance of recruiting high quality, professional staff.
- The Rhiya Malin case highlights the legal implications for settings. Both Casterbridge Nursery and Kayley Murphy, who was on her mobile phone when she should have been supervising Rhiya, were prosecuted and fined separately.
- Meeting staff:child ratios is not sufficient to guarantee children's safety. Staff must be committed, passionate professionals.

Key lessons

Risk assessment re-visited

The accident analysis in this book has shown defects in risk assessment to be the second highest factor in accident and incident causation. This has included:

- a failure to make an adequate assessment of risks
- a failure to action control measures identified through risk assessment.

From the data available it is difficult to identify why this may have occurred. Failure to make an adequate risk assessment may be a result of the competence of the person completing the risk assessment or perhaps a failure to recognise a specific risk, or confusion about what a risk assessment entails and what it should contain. Keep your risk assessments simple and relevant. Concentrate on 'real' and not insignificant or fanciful risks. Sometimes, in trying to cover every eventuality in a risk assessment, the significant risks can be missed. There is advice and guidance including model risk assessments on the HSE website at www.hse.gov.uk.

Again, involve your staff in the risk assessment process. They have a good knowledge of the business and will know where the problems are. If you decide to engage a consultant to assist you in this process, then ensure that they are competent. The HSE has a register of Occupational Safety and Health Consultants known as the OSHCR, available on the website at www.hse.gov.uk. If you decide to use a consultant to assist you in your risk assessments, it is still important that you and your staff are involved and have an input into this process. You know your business and your premises better than they do.

Failing to take action on a significant risk identified in your risk assessment where existing control measures are inadequate is unacceptable. It is important that you use your risk assessments to plan your safety priorities. If your risk assessment identifies that something is 'high risk' then you need to deal with this first. In the example of the finger trapping accident that occurred at the special needs school, the local authority failed to deal with the known and identified risk. While the control measure of supervision was put in place, this was inadequate and impractical as a long-term solution. Use an action plan to keep track of any actions required to be undertaken as a result of your risk assessments.

Back to the team

- Look at the statements made in your setting's publicity material.
- What are you promising to deliver in your setting?
- Is everyone delivering the quality you are promising?
- How do you know? What evidence do you have to support your opinions?

Train your staff

Providing your staff with information, instruction, training and supervision is not only a moral responsibility, it is also the law. Staff need to know what is expected of them and they need to have the knowledge, ability and attributes to do their job properly. The Cameron Lindsay case is an example of where an inadequately qualified and inexperienced staff member had been left in charge of a setting. This not only presents a dangerous practice but it is also grossly unfair on the individual. The cases where children have sustained finger entrapment injuries highlight the need for common sense to guide risk assessments. Babies and young children are innately active, inquisitive and driven to explore their environment. Doors of every description always seem to hold a fascination with children, as they enjoy the repetition of opening and closing them. As children develop, their ability to move with speed and climb on equipment and furniture can pose a challenge for staff caring for children. Supervision is vital. Qualifications and experience can help with understanding about children's developing needs. However, common sense also plays a huge part in anticipating and removing hazards.

Key lessons

> ### Key point ⚏
>
> - Qualifications do not always equate to common sense.

First aid

Many cases have highlighted how children have been treated by staff whose first aid certificates had expired. The Statutory Framework for the EYFS requirements regarding first aid are only the minimum standards that settings need to adhere to. High quality settings have always ensured that ongoing professional development and training for staff includes keeping their first aid skills and training up to date. In the Georgia Hollick case, the qualified first aider was supervising sleeping children and shouted instructions to staff who were trying to treat Georgia. The The Statutory Framework for the EYFS states that providers consider the deployment of staff by taking into account the layout of the building, to ensure children can receive prompt treatment, as a minimum.

> ### Key point ⚏
>
> - New guidelines regarding first aid for nursery and pre-school staff are due to come into force from September 2016 as a result of the campaign led by Joanne and Dan Thompson, whose daughter Millie choked to death in 2012.

 Back to the team

- Are you meeting the minimum requirements for first aid in your setting, all day, every day?
- Who monitors the expiry dates on first aid certificates?

Equipment

The cases where children have died or been injured because of equipment were mainly due to:

- equipment not being suitable for the age range
- equipment being modified, such as attaching a rope to a climbing frame
- failure to risk assess before use or an inadequate risk assessment
- manufacturers' instructions being ignored
- failure to take defective equipment out of use.

You must carefully consider the equipment that you bring into the premises for use by the children in your care. You have a responsibility to select equipment that is safe and suitable for use. You also need to carry out a risk assessment before taking the equipment into use. Equipment needs to be maintained and you must check that it remains in good condition and safe to use. It may be tempting to modify play equipment to enhance learning and play value but this is fraught with danger and should not be done without liaising with the supplier or provider and making sure that it is safe to do so. Suppliers are unlikely to validate this in terms of safety as they will not have control over your modifications and how they are carried out.

Always read and follow the manufacturer's instructions. These instructions are provided for a purpose so if they limit the age range of the children for whom the equipment has been designed for use, you must comply with these guidelines. Likewise if it is stated that 'children should not be left unattended in the equipment' you must comply with this also. In the case of Cameron Lindsay, the manufacturer's instructions to ensure children were always supervised when using the cradle were clearly ignored.

Key points ⚷

- If you do not read the manufacturer's instructions, then vital safety advice can be missed.
- Staff need to take seriously the safety instructions on the inspection of equipment and how to deal with defective equipment. Checks need to be completed with diligence. They must never be just a paperwork exercise.

Premises

The provision of a safe place to work is another legal requirement under health and safety legislation. The requirement to ensure the health and safety of others affected by your business activity extends this requirement to providing a safe environment for children in your care. The accidents and incidents that we analysed were a result of:

- a lack of safety equipment such as finger guards
- unsafe premises (exposure to ACMs due to remedial work)
- access to areas not intended for use by children, but inadequate restrictions in place.

The number of serious injuries resulting from finger trapping incidents is quite shocking, as is the failure to take action to address this hazard when it had been identified in risk assessment. This has long been a recognised hazard in premises, particularly those occupied by vulnerable people, such as children. The good news is that the British Standards Institute (BSI) has set up a committee to write a standard for safety devices that can be used to safely address this hazard and to stop these preventable injuries. Hazards in your workplace should be identified through your risk assessments. It is important to think about the hazard from a child's perspective. What may not pose a significant risk to an adult could result in an accident to a child.

Parents' advice/children's needs ignored

The Statutory Framework for the EYFS is clear that working in partnership with parents and/or carers is crucial in supporting staff to meet children's individual needs. It is one of the four overarching principles of the EYFS. Parents know their children best and can alert staff to developmental changes. In the case of Molly Cunliffe, her parents had specifically warned staff that Molly had started to put things around her neck. This advice was ignored when Molly was put to sleep in a cot with a drawstring bag hanging on it. Molly subsequently strangled herself on the cord of the bag.

Key points

- It is crucial to listen to parents and/or carers and act on their expert knowledge of their own children.
- Parents and/or carers may request specific guidance to be followed, especially around feeding their children. Some children can be fussy eaters and require gentle encouragement and patience at mealtimes. Others have specific dietary needs and/or allergies and it is crucial that all staff know, understand and implement any restrictions that this may entail. In the case of Georgia Hollick, she was given a piece of fruit while sitting on the floor and subsequently choked to death. This was despite her parents requesting that Georgia be fed in a high chair. Did staff blatantly ignore her parents' request for Georgia to be fed in a high chair or had this information not been passed onto all staff?
- In the case of Thomas Egan, his mother had informed the nursery of his milk allergy. Unfortunately, Thomas was fed a milk-based cereal for breakfast and subsequently died from anaphylactic shock. It is crucial that communication systems in settings are effective in ensuring that all staff are aware of children's specific needs and parents' specific requests for how their children need to be cared for.

- What type of requests do parents make about their children's specific care needs?

- Think about the initial meeting you have with parents and/or carers. What reassurances are you offering about how their children will be cared for?

- Review and evaluate how information is communicated with the team.

Back to the team

There is another issue here with regard to hanging drawstring bags on cots. It probably made the baby room look more attractive.

- Do you have anything in your setting that cosmetically makes a room/area look inviting and attractive?
- Look at it again: Does it pose a risk to children?

Poor food hygiene practice

Poor food hygiene practices and dirty food premises not only contravene food law but also can lead to cases of food poisoning, foodborne illnesses and outbreaks of gastrointestinal infections in a setting. Like health and safety, food safety needs to be managed as an integral part of the business and needs to be taken seriously. Food poisoning and foodborne illnesses can be fatal in young children and/or can lead to serious long-term health effects. If you prepare and serve food in a setting, you are a food business operator and you have a legal duty to provide food that is safe to eat.

Reflection

- What does a safe, responsible workplace look like to you?

- What role do you play in that safe, responsible work place?

- Evaluate what needs to be done differently to ensure that minimum standards are not just met, but exceeded.

Key lessons

149

Final thoughts

> Reflection is key in helping individuals understand what they would do differently next time. As practitioners, we need to take reflexive action in order to try and prevent future, avoidable accidents.

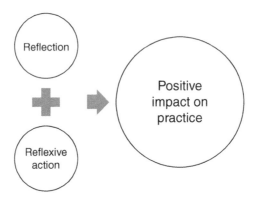

In conclusion, we would like to make an observation and express concern about the lack of readily available statistics relating to accidents and incidents in early years settings. We have placed much emphasis in this book on the importance of providers investigating accidents, learning from mistakes and reviewing practice to try to prevent recurrence. The Statutory Framework for the EYFS requires that all serious accidents, illnesses, injuries or the death of a child while in the care of a setting must be notified to Ofsted and the local child protection agencies. Notifications need to be made as soon as is reasonably practicable, but within 14 days of any situation arising.

There are separate requirements under RIDDOR 2013 with differing timescales, but these apply to deaths, injuries, illnesses and incidents affecting employees and specifically death or reportable injuries to 'non workers'. During the consultation in 2012 on changes to RIDDOR 1995, there was a proposal to remove the reporting requirement for non-fatal accidents to persons not at work (www.hse.gov.uk).

This proposal would have meant that a serious accident such as happened to Eshan Ahmed would not have required reporting to the enforcing authority under RIDDOR. Fortunately, this proposal was rejected in the consultation process and the requirement remains in RIDDOR 2013. Information from RIDDOR is collated by the HSE, which produces annual statistics concerning workplace accidents, ill health and dangerous occurrences. It is worth remembering here that these statistics in relation to childcare settings and the children as 'non workers' will only relate to *deaths and non-fatal injuries where the injured person was taken from site to hospital for treatment*. There is a range of other serious injuries that will not require notification under RIDDOR because the injured child was not taken to hospital from site for treatment.

The HSE has used its accident statistics to highlight and target campaigns aimed at improving health and safety by dealing with specific industries and risks. A recent campaign called 'safer sites' is based on the construction industry. Using information from accident/incident data helps to focus resources and allows for key targeted and consistent interventions and advice. In another campaign, the HSE highlighted the risks of occupational dermatitis in a number of sectors including hospitality and catering, hairdressing, florists and construction.

What analysis Ofsted undertakes with regard to the data that it collects from its notification process is unclear to us. Ofsted was unable to accommodate our freedom of information (FoI) request for '*information about notifications made to them by early years and childcare settings of any serious accident, illness or injury to, or death of any child or any incident/near misses while in their care, dating back to 2000*'. Ofsted highlighted that there are over 76,000 registered childcare providers required to conform with the requirements of the Statutory Framework for the EYFS, including the notification process. Inspectors may carry out 'priority inspections' – point 8 of the Inspection handbook refers to how a priority inspection may be generated because a provider has made a notification.

Ofsted makes a distinction between an inspector carrying out an inspection and not investigating the subject matter of a notification. However, Inspectors are required to pursue lines of enquiry around the notification and use this evidence to form part of the overall judgement for the inspection. Lines of enquiry include 'whether the incident was preventable, any lessons learned and subsequent action taken to reduce risks' (Ofsted, Early years inspection handbook, May 2015, p6. www.gov.uk). Our response letter from Ofsted, highlighted to extract the information we requested, would require a manual review of each notification and this would be too costly under the time constraints of the FoI Act.

Ofsted's own notification process is best placed to be collating accident data or referring data on for analysis to another department/authority, as possibly five individuals (admin, CIE team member, inspector, inspectors' team manager, quality assurance manager) within Ofsted can have sight of this information. This is shown in the flowchart below.

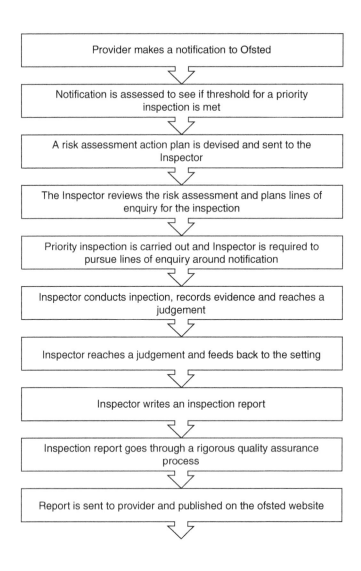

As part of the report writing process, Ofsted inspectors are required to include the numbers of children and services provided in order for this information to be collated for statistical purposes. We think it is imperative that data about notifications, such as whether incidents were preventable, any lessons learned and subsequent action taken to reduce risks, are also collated. It is only by collecting and analysing data that trends can be identified, information can be shared among providers and improvements can be made.

 Back to the team

'If people were aware of what is at stake during the first few years of life, small children would be society's treasures' (Rosa Maria Torres).

Summary of changes that have affected all aspects of caring for children

Date	Guidance/Legislation
1998	Data Protection Act (DPA) 1998
1989	The Children Act 1989
1996	Day Care and Childminding (National Standards implemented (England) Regulations 2003 No.1996, and other regulations under Part XA of the Children Act 1989
1996	National Curriculum for the pre-school sector who would be claiming voucher status Desirable Outcomes, (SCAA 1996) published
1997	Nursery Education Voucher scheme for four-year-olds implemented
1997	Publication of a significant white paper, Excellence in Schools (DfEE, 1997)
1999	Early Learning Goals guidance (QCA) published
2000	Freedom of Information Act
2001	Ofsted Inspections for early years and childcare settings
2002	Education Act 2002
2002	*Birth to Three Matters* published
2003	*Every Child Matters* (ECM) a UK government initiative for England and Wales that was launched in 2003, at least partly in response to the death of Victoria Climbié
2003	Education (School Teachers' Prescribed Qualifications, etc.) Order 2003 Educations (School Teachers Qualifications) (England) Regulations 2003
2004	The Children Act 2004 incorporated recommendations from the Lord Laming review following the death of Victoria Climbié in 2000
2004	First children's commissioner appointed. Local Safeguarding Children Boards (LSCB) established
2004	Bichard inquiry into the deaths of Holly Wells and Jessica Chapman resulted in the tightening up of Criminal Record checks and Safer Recruitment guidance issued
2006	The Childcare Act 2006
2006	Safeguarding Vulnerable Groups Act 2006
2007	Death of Peter Connolly, Lord Laming conducted another review
2007	The Early Years Foundation Stage (Learning and Development Requirements) Order 2007
2008	The Childcare (Exemptions from Registration) Order
2008	Childcare (Early Years Register) Regulations 2008
2009	Childcare (disqualification) Regulations
2009	Childcare (Provision of information About Young Children) (England) Regulations 2009
2012	Disclosure and Barring Service (DBS) formed by merging the functions of the Criminal Records Bureau (CRB) and the Independent Safeguarding Authority (ISA) under the Protection of Freedoms Act 2012
2012	Childcare (Early Years Register) (Amendment) Regulations 2012

2012	The Early Years Foundation Stage (Welfare Requirements) Regulations 2012, as amended. Introduction of the prime and specific areas of learning
2012	Development Matters introduced
2012	Progress Check at age 2 introduced
2012	Funding for disadvantaged families with two-year-olds introduced with entitlement extended in 2013 and 2014
2013	Development Matters replaced by Early Years outcomes
2013	Early Years Teachers Standards introduced
2013	Early Tears Educator (level 3) qualification criteria introduced
2013	Early Years Initial Teacher Training commenced
2014	Children and Families Act 2014
2014	Childcare (Welfare & Registration Requirements) Amendment
2014	The Statutory Framework for the Early Years Foundation Stage September 2014 updated version published
2014	Progress Check at age 2 and EYFS profile updated guidance
2014	SEND Code of Practice (11/06/14)
2015	Early Years Pupil Premium (EYPP) piloted by six local authorities, ready to be rolled out later in the year
2015	SEND Code of Practice Updated (01/05/15)
2015	The Integrated Review at Age Two came in September 2015, bringing together the EYFS Progress Check at age 2 with the Healthy Child Programme (HCP) 2–2½ year health and development review, into an integrated process
2015	Early Years Educator (level 3) qualification requirements revised
2015	Fundamental British Values incorporated into inspections of early years providers
2015	Common inspection framework for early years introduced in September 2015

List of abbreviations

ACM	Asbestos containing materials
BCPA	British Pest Control Association
BSI	British Standards Institute
CAPT	Child Accident Prevention Trust
CBT	Children's Burns Trust
CCR	Childcare Register (Compulsory)
CPD	Continuing Professional Development
CPS	Crown Prosecution Service
CRB	Criminal Records Bureau
DBS	Disclosure and Barring Service
DfE	Department for Education
DPA	Data Protection Act
DSS	Door Safety Standard
ECM	Every Child Matters
EU	European Union
EYFS	Early Years Foundation Stage
EYP	Early Years Professional
EYPP	Early Years Pupil Premium
EYR	Early Years Register
FoI	Freedom of information
FSA	Food Standards Agency
GP	General Practitioner
HACCP	Hazard Analysis Critical Control Point
HPA	Health Protection Agency
HSE	Health and Safety Executive
HUS	Haemolytic uraemic syndrome
ISA	Independent Safeguarding Authority
LA	Local Authority
LADO	Local Authority Designated Officer
LSCB	Local Safeguarding Children Board
MBC	Metropolitan Borough Council
NPTA	National Pest Technicians Association
Ofsted	Office for Standards in Education
ONS	Office for National Statistics
QCA	Qualifications and Curriculum Authority
RIDDOR	Reporting of Injuries, Diseases and Dangerous Occurrences Regulations (2013)
RoSPA	Royal Society for the Prevention of Accidents
SEND	Special Educational Needs and Disabilities
VCR	Childcare Register (Voluntary)
VTEC	Vero cytotoxin-producing Escherichia coli
WHO	World Health Organisation

Bibliography

This book contains public sector information licensed under the Open Government Licence vs. http://www.nationalarchives.gov.uk/doc/open-government-licence/.

This includes public sector information published by the HSE and licensed under the Open Government License v3.0.

Allergies: http://www.allergyuk.org (accessed 6 May 2015)

Anaphylaxis: http://www.anaphylaxis.org.uk (accessed 6 May 2015)

Asbestos: http://www.beware-asbestos.info (accessed 6 May 2015)

Asbestos: http://www.punchline-gloucester.com/articles/december2014/cheltenhamchildrensnurseryprosecutedafterasbestosexposure

Asbestos: http://www.cheltenham.gov.uk/news/article/1166/a_cheltenham_business_and_contractor_prosecuted_after_asbestos_Exposure)

Ahmed, E. case: http://www.telegraph.co.uk/education/educationnews/9562575/Nursery-fined-over-cover-up-after-fall-left-child-in-a-coma.html (accessed 6 May 2015)

Baker, S. http://www.newsshopper.co.uk/news/4402651.CHELSFIELD____40_000_fine_after_nursery_salmonella_outbreak/ (accessed 6 May 2015)

BBC: http://news.bbc.co.uk/1/hi/england/london/4514402.stm (accessed 6 May 2015)

BBC: http://news.bbc.co.uk/1/hi/england/bristol/4218646.stm (accessed 6 May 2015)

BBC: http://www.bbc.co.uk/news/uk-england-manchester-25232661 (accessed 6 May 2015)

BBC: http://www.bbc.co.uk/news/uk-england-essex-23100844 accessed 6 May 2015)

BBC: http://news.bbc.co.uk/1/hi/england/london/6599825.stm (accessed 6 May 2015)

BBC: http://news.bbc.co.uk/go/pr/fr/-/hi/england/beds/bucks/herts/3226675.stm (accessed 6 May 2015)

BBC: http://www.bbc.co.uk/news/uk-england-norfolk-16288570 (accessed 6 May 2015)

BBC: http://news.bbc.co.uk/go/pr/fr/-/1/hi/england/london/8399514.stm (accessed 6 May 2015)

BBC: http://news.bbc.co.uk/go/pr/fr/-/1/hi/england/coventry_warwickshire/4837614.stm (accessed 6 May 2015)

BBC: http://news.bbc.co.uk/1/hi/england/london/8399514.stm (accessed 6 May 2015)

BBC: http://news.bbc.co.uk/1/hi/england/7747854.stm (accessed 6 May 2015)

Berlin, B. http://www.telegraph.co.uk/Education/Educationnews/9562575/Nursery-fined-over-cover-up-after-fall-left-child-in-a-coma.html (accessed 6 May 2015)

Birmingham Magistrates: http://www.birminghammail.co.uk/news/local-news/nursery-guilt-over-tots-scalding-41331) (accessed 6 May 2015)

Birmingham Mail: http://www.birminghammail.co.uk/news/local-news/fine-for-mice-infested-birmingham-nursery-161394 (accessed 6 May 2015)

Bishop, L. case: http://www.nurseryworld.co.uk/nursery-world/news/1141957/york-college-nursery-lydia-bishops-death-completely-avoidable (accessed 6 May 2015)

Bishop, L. case: Coulson, J: 'R v York College, Leeds Crown Court 14 February 2014 Sentencing Remarks of Coulson J' https://www.judiciary.gov.uk/wp-content/uploads/JCO/Documents/Judgments/r-v-york-college.pdf (accessed 24 October 2015)

Brooker, F. case: http://www.dailymail.co.uk/news/article-2602344/Parents-threatened-having-15-month-old-daughter-taken-away-social-services-suffers-unexplainable-burns-blisters-fingers-NURSERY.html (accessed 6 May 2015)

Busby. L. case: http://www.hullcc.gov.uk/portal/page?_pageid=221,674011&_dad=portal&_schema=PORTAL&p_id=4847 (accessed 6 May 2015)

Cannock House Day Nursery: http://www.newsshopper.co.uk/news/4402651.CHELSFIELD____40_000_fine_after_nursery_salmonella_outbreak/

Campylobacter guide: http://www.food.gov.uk/news-updates/campaigns/campylobacter/fsw-2014

CAPT: http://www.capt.org.uk/who-we-are/news/bbc-highlights-dangers-button-batteries-one-show (accessed 6 May 2015)

CAPT: http://www.capt.org.uk/resources/talking-about-strangulationpdf (accessed 6 May 2015)

CAPT ongoing safety campaigns: http://www.capt.org.uk/?gclid=CMeDj6aSrcUCFSLlwgod_AwA2w (accessed 6 May 2015)

CAPT: http://capt.org.uk/what-we-do/training-consultancy-mentoring/consultancy-services/targeted-awareness-campaigns (accessed 6 May 2015)

CAPT: http://www.capt.org.uk/safety-advice/keeping-your-child-safe-drowning) (accessed 6 May 2015)

CAPT: http://www.capt.org.uk/resources/drowning (accessed 6 May 2015)

CAPT: http://www.capt.org.uk/safety-advice/protecting-your-child-burns-and-scalds (accessed 6 May 2015)

CB Trust: http://www.cbtrust.org.uk/ (accessed 6 May 2015)

Chauhan, T. case: http://www.dailymail.co.uk/news/article-2202297/Dicky-Birds-nursery-Police-investigate-death-year-old-Tiya-Chauhan-choked-jelly-cube.html (accessed 6 May 2015)

CIEH Chartered Institute of Environmental Health Publication, 'Pest Control Procedures in the Food Industry': http://www.cieh.org/uploadedfiles/core/policy/publications_and_information_services/policy_publications/publications/pest_control_food_industry.pdf (accessed 22 May 2015)

CIEH Chartered Institute of Environmental Health (CIEH) report: Regina v Cannock Day Nursery Limited: http://www.cieh.org/uploadedFiles/Core/Membership/Regional_network/London/News_and_Events/Perspectives-Case-Study.pdf (accessed 23 May 2015)

Childalert: http://www.childalert.co.uk/safety.php?tab=Safety (accessed 6 May 2015)

Children's Charter: http://www.childrens-charter.org/index.html)

Coeliac: https://www.coeliac.org.uk/home/ (accessed 6 May 2015)

Coroners' Reports: https://www.gov.uk/government/uploads/system/uploads/attachment_data/file/217348/summary-rule-43–070312.pdf (accessed 6 May 2015)

Coventry Telegraph, Dosanjh, D. case: http://www.coventrytelegraph.net/news/coventry-news/coventry-school-staffs-fight-save-3035168 (accessed 29 May 2015)

Cheltenham City Council: http://www.cheltenham.gov.uk/news/article/1166/a_cheltenham_business_and_contractor_prosecuted_after_asbestos_Exposure (accessed 6 May 2015)

Crew Chronicle: http://www.crewechronicle.co.uk/news/local-news/nursery-fined-10000-after-girl-5635077 http://www.cheltenham.gov.uk/news/article/1166/a_cheltenham_business_and_contractor_prosecuted_after_asbestos_Exposure (accessed 6 May 2015)

Churchley, P. http://www.getsurrey.co.uk/news/nursery-fined-after-two-year-old-boy-6520361 (accessed 6 May 2015)

Cunliffe, M. case http://news.bbc.co.uk/1/hi/england/gloucestershire/6273602.stm (accessed 6 May 2015)

Daily Mail: http://www.dailymail.co.uk/news/article-2358766/Mother-sues-nursery-staff-spilt-burning-CHICKEN-FAT-year-old-son-leaving-second-degree-burns.html (accessed 6 May 2015)

Daily Mail: http://www.dailymail.co.uk/news/article-2602344/Parents-threatened-having-15-month-old-daughter-taken-away-social-services-suffers-unexplainable-burns-blisters-fingers-NURSERY.html (accessed 6 May 2015)

Daily Mail, autism case: http://www.dailymail.co.uk/news/article-2970633/Girl-13-suffered-rare-form-autism-choked-death-meatball-school-canteen.html (accessed 6 May 2015)

Daily Mail: http://www.dailymail.co.uk/news/article-2124043/Chantelle-Firth-Pentland-Primary-School-student-6-dies-choking-lunch.html (accessed 6 May 2015)

Drowning: http://drowningpreventionweek.org.uk/ (accessed 6 May 2015)

Early years outcomes: https://www.gov.uk/government/publications/early-years-outcomes (accessed 6 May 2015)

E. coli case: http://www.bbc.co.uk/news/uk-england-merseyside-28152470

E. coli case: http://www.bbc.co.uk/news/uk-england-tees-32732974

E. coli case: http://www.bournemouthecho.co.uk/news/11625959.UPDATE__Council_nursery_closes_its_doors_after_E_coll_outbreak_hospitalises_pre_school_children/?ref=mr (accessed 6 May 2015)

E. coli case: http://www.dailymail.co.uk/health/article-149458/Nursery-youngsters-battle-E-coli-bug.html (accessed 6 May 2015)

E. coli case: http://www.eastbourneherald.co.uk/news/local/e-coli-outbreak-closes-hellingly-nursery-1-1435379 (accessed 6 May 2015)

E. coli case: http://www.lancashiretelegraph.co.uk/news/11562242.Two_children_in_hospital_following_E_coll_outbreak_at_East_Lancs_nursery/?ref=rss (accessed 6 May 2015)

E. coli case: http://www.theguardian.com/uk/2006/may/14/health.healthandwellbeing (accessed 6 May 2015)

E. coli case: http://news.stv.tv/north/193121-child-left-blind-and-deaf-following-ecoli-outbreak-at-nursery/ (accessed 6 May 2015)

E. coli case: http://www.nurseryworld.co.uk/nursery-world/news/1081752/study-puffins-pre-school-brecon-wales (accessed 6 May 2015)

E. coli case: http://www.manchestereveningnews.co.uk/news/greater-manchester-news/ecoli-probe-at-nursery-930229 (accessed 6 May 2015)

E. coli case: http://www.wales.nhs.uk/sitesplus/862/news/20701 (accessed 6 May 2015)

E. coli case: http://www.walesonline.co.uk/news/local-news/nursery-playgroup-re-open-after-bangor-1797949 (accessed 6 May 2015)

E. coli guide: https://www.food.gov.uk/business-industry/guidancenotes/hygguid/ecoliguide

EC Regulation No. 852/2004 On the hygiene of foodstuffs: http://eur-lex.europa.eu/legal-content/EN/TXT/?uri=uriserv:OJ.L_.2004.226.01.0003.01.ENG (accessed 23/10/15

Egan, T. case: http://news.bbc.co.uk/1/hi/england/2702111.stm (accessed 6 May 2015)

Eisenhower, Dwight D., American President: http://dying.about.com/od/thegrievingprocess/a/Grief-Quotes-Children.htm (accessed 6 May 2015)

EU Food Information for Consumers Regulation (No. 1169/2011): http://eur-lex.europa.eu/legal-content/EN/TXT/?uri=celex:32011R1169 (accessed 23/10/15)

European Child Safety Alliance, Childhood falls, October 2009: http://www.childsafetyeurope.org/publications/info/factsheets/childhood-falls.pdf

Evening Standard: http://www.standard.co.uk/news/nursery-admits-guilt-over-baby-death-6986169.html (accessed 6 May 2015)

DfE, Statutory Framework for the Early Years Foundation Stage. London

https://www.gov.uk/government/uploads/system/uploads/attachment_data/file/335504/EYFS_framework_from_1_September_2014__with_clarification_note.pdf (accessed 21 october 2015)

Farm Visits, 'Visit my Farm' Industry code of practice: http://www.visitmyfarm.org/component/k2/item/339-industry-code-of-practice (accessed 25 May 2015)

Farrel, H. case: http://www.dailymail.co.uk/news/article-2358766/Mother-sues-nursery-staff-spilt-burning-CHICKEN-FAT-year-old-son-leaving-second-degree-burns.html (accessed 6 May 2015)

Food Safety Act 1990 (as amended): http://www.legislation.gov.uk/ukpga/1990/16/contents (accessed 23.10.15)

Food safety: http://www.foodsafety.gov/keep/basics/ads/index.html (accessed 25 May 2015)

Food Standards Agency (FSA): http://allergytraining.food.gov.uk/english/food-allergy-facts.aspx (accessed 6 May 2015)

Food Standards Agency (FSA): https://www.food.gov.uk/sites/default/files/multimedia/pdfs/publication/loosefoodsleaflet.pdf (accessed 6 May 2015)

Food Standards Agency (FSA): https://www.food.gov.uk/sites/default/files/multimedia/pdfs/publication/allergy-labelling-prepacked.pdf (accessed 6 May 2015)

Food Standards Agency (FSA): https://www.food.gov.uk/sites/default/files/multimedia/pdfs/publication/allergencontrollaeho1208.pdf (accessed 6 May 2015)

Food Standards Agency (FSA): https://www.food.gov.uk/enforcement/enforcetrainfund/onlinetraining/allergytraining (accessed 6 May 2015)

Food Standards Agency (FSA): https://www.food.gov.uk/news-updates/news/allergy-alerts-news (accessed 6 May 2015)

Food Standards Agency (FSA): https://www.food.gov.uk/news-updates/campaigns (accessed 23 May 2015)

Food Standards Agency (FSA): http://www.food.gov.uk/news- Food Standards Agency (FSA): updates/campaigns/campylobacter/fsw-2014 (accessed 22 May 2015)

Food Standards Agency (FSA): Food Standards Agency Outbreak Management, 'Management of outbreaks of foodborne illness in England and Wales': http://www.food.gov.uk/sites/default/files/multimedia/pdfs/outbreakmanagement.pdf (accessed 23 May 2015)

Garvey, D. and Lancaster, A., *Leadership for Quality in Early Years and Playwork,* 2010, National children's Bureau, London

Get Surrey: http://www.getsurrey.co.uk/news/surrey-news/godstone-farm-ecoli-outbreak---7059615 (accessed 6 May 2015)

Get Surrey: http://www.getsurrey.co.uk/news/nursery-fined-after-two-year-old-boy-6520361 (accessed 6 May 2015)

Greenfield, J. http://www.getsurrey.co.uk/news/surrey-news/godstone-farm-ecoli-outbreak---7059615) (accessed 6 May 2015)

GOV.UK: https://www.gov.uk/government/uploads/system/uploads/attachment_data/file/342361/Review_of_major_outbreak_of_E_coli_o157_in_surrey_2009.pdf (accessed 6 May 2015)

GOV.UK: https://www.gov.uk/notifiable-diseases-and-causative-organisms-how-to-report (accessed 6 May 2015)

GOV.UK: https://www.gov.uk/government/publications/escherichia-coli-e-coli-o157-report-and-recommendations-from-2009-godstone-incident (accessed 6 May 2015)

GOV.UK: https://www.gov.uk/tuberculosis-screening (accessed 6 May 2015)

Health and Safety Executive (HSE) http://www.hse.gov.uk/ (accessed 23.10.15)

HSE Asbestos: http://www.hse.gov.uk/asbestos/ (accessed 6 May 2015)

HSE, E. coli: http://www.hse.gov.uk/campaigns/farmsafe/ecoli.htm (accessed 6 May 2015)

HSE, First aid: http://www.hse.gov.uk/firstaid/ (accessed 6 May 2015)

HSE, First aid: http://www.hse.gov.uk/pubns/books/l74.htm (accessed 23 May 2015)

HSE, Inquests: http://www.hse.gov.uk/enforce/enforcementguide/wrdeaths/chronology.htm (accessed 6 May 2015)

HSE, Investigating accidents: http://www.hse.gov.uk/managing/delivering/check/investigating-accidents-incidents.htm (accessed 6 May 2015)

HSE, Managing: http://www.hse.gov.uk/managing/plan-do-check-act.htm (accessed 23 May 2015)

HSE, Myth: http://www.hse.gov.uk/myth/september.htm (accessed 6 May 2015)

HSE, Prosecution Leapfrog Nursery: http://www.hse.gov.uk/lau/pdfs/lauprosecutions0708.pdf (accessed 6 May 2015)

HSE Publication http://www.hse.gov.uk/pubns/books/hsg48.htm (accessed 25 May 2015)

HSE Publiction: http://www.hse.gov.uk/pubns/books/hsg65.htm (accessed 25 May 2015)

HSE Publication: http://www.hse.gov.uk/pubns/indg223.pdf (accessed 6 May 2015)

HSE Publication: http://www.hse.gov.uk/pubns/hsg245.pdf (accessed 23 May 2015)

HSE Publication: http://www.hse.gov.uk/pubns/indg345.pdf (accessed 23 May 2015)

HSE Publication: http://www.hse.gov.uk/pubns/indg453.pdf (accessed 23 May 2015)

HSERIDDOR: http://www.hse.gov.uk/riddor/ (accessed 23 May 2015)

HSE, Risk: http://www.hse.gov.uk/Risk/ (accessed 6 May 2015)

HSESalford Prosecution: http://press.hse.gov.uk/2014/salford-council-prosecuted-after-child-loses-fingertips-in-school-gate/?ebul=hsegen&cr=10/14-apr-14 (accessed 6 May 2015)

HSE, School trips: http://www.hse.gov.uk/services/education/school-trips.htm (accessed 6 May 2015)

HSE, Training: http://www.hse.gov.uk/pubns/indg345.pdf (accessed 6 May 2015)

Health and Safety at Work Etc. Act 1974 http://www.legislation.gov.uk/ukpga/1974/37 (accessed 23.10.15)

Health and Safety (First Aid) Regulations 1981 http://www.legislation.gov.uk/uksi/1981/917/contents/made (accessed 23/10/15)

Health Protection Agency Review of the major outbreak of E. coli 0157 in Surrey 2009: Report of the Independent Investigation Committee June 2010 https://www.gov.uk/government/

uploads/system/uploads/attachment_data/file/342361/Review_of_major_outbreak_of_E_coll_o157_in_surrey_2009.pdf (accessed 23.10.15)

Hearsey, R. http://news.bbc.co.uk/go/pr/fr/-/1/hi/england/coventry_warwickshire/4837614.stm (accessed 6 May 2015)

Hewitt, J. http://www.hullcc.gov.uk?portal/page?_pageid=221,674011&_dad=potal&_scheme (accessed 6 May 2015).

Hollick, G. case: http://www.telegraph.co.uk/news/uknews/4969646/Nursery-company-fined-145000-for-baby-choking-death.html (accessed 6 May 2015)

Holt, S. case: http://vscg.co.uk/case-law/stamford_park_hse_prosecution

Hull County Council: http://www.hullcc.gov.uk?portal/page?_pageid=221,674011&_dad=potal&_scheme (accessed 6 May 2015)

Hunt, M. case: http://www.birminghammail.co.uk/news/local-news/nursery-guilt-over-tots-scalding-41331 (accessed 6 May 2015)

Independent: http://www.independent.co.uk/news/uk/this-britain/nursery-is-fined-60000-over-death-of-allergic-baby-93930.html (accessed 6 May 2015)

Infection control: https://www.gov.uk/government/uploads/system/uploads/attachment_data/file/353953/Guidance_on_infection_control_in_schools_11_Sept.pdf (accessed 6 May 2015)

Ladwa, O. case: http://www.dailymail.co.uk/news/article-450954/Toddler-crushed-death-ambulance-thought-warnings-game.html (accessed 6 May 2015)

Last, A. http://www.birminghammail.co.uk/news/local-news/fine-for-mice-infested-birmingham-nursery-161394)

Lindsay, C. case: http://news.bbc.co.uk/1/hi/england/hereford/worcs/4887892.stm (accessed 6 May 2015)

Make it safe: http://www.makeitsafe.org.uk (accessed 6 May 2015)

Malin, R. case: http://www.dailymail.co.uk/news/article-1336141/Rhiya-Malin-2-died-heart-attack-getting-head-stuck-window.html (accessed 6 May 2015)

Malin, R. case: http://www.bbc.co.uk/news/uk-england-essex-23100844 (accessed 6 May 2015)

(The) Management of Health and Safety at Work Regulations 1999 http://www.legislation.gov.uk/uksi/1999/3242/contents/made (accessed 23/10/15)

Milner, A. case: http://www.dailymail.co.uk/news/article-1232942/Toddler-dies-choking-sausage-nursery.html#ixzz27Pcs8Xu6 (accessed 6 May 2015)

Millie's Campaign: https://www.gov.uk/government/news/first-aid-training-to-be-made-compulsory-for-new-nursery-recruits (accessed 6 May 2015)

Morse, M. http://www.telegraph.co.uk/Education/Educationnews/9562575/Nursery-fined-over-cover-up-after-fall-left-child-in-a-coma.html (accessed 6 May 2015)

Newcastle: http://www.newcastle.gov.uk/business/trading-standards/campaigns/safety-of-button-cell-batteries (accessed 6 May 2015)

Newshopper: http://www.newsshopper.co.uk/news/4402651.CHELSFIELD_____40_000_fine_after_nursery_salmonella_outbreak/ (accessed 6 May 2015)

NHS: http://www.patientsafetyfirst.nhs.uk/ashx/Asset.ashx?path=/Intervention-support/FALLSHow-to%20Guide%20v4.pdf (accessed 6 May 2015)

NHS: http://www.nhs.uk/Conditions/Burns-and-scalds/Pages/Introduction.aspx

NICE: https://www.nice.org.uk/guidance/cg117 (accessed 6 May 2015)

Nursery World: C. Gaunt, 14 January 2013. http://www.nurseryworld.co.uk/nursery-world/news/1097515/exclusive-concern-lack-nursery-deaths-injuries (accessed 6 May 2015)

Nursery World: http://www.nurseryworld.co.uk/nursery-world/news/1146441/nursery-grossly-negligent-inquest-child-death (accessed 6 May 2015)

Nursery World: http://www.nurseryworld.co.uk/nursery-world/news/1105400/newborns-vaccinated-tb (accessed 6 May 2015)

Ofsted, CIE handbook: https://www.gov.uk/government/publications/compliance-investigation-and-enforcement-handbook-childcare (accessed 6 May 2015)

Ofsted, Early years inspection handbook. No 102101: https://www.gov.uk/government/uploads/system/uploads/attachment_data/file/429502/Early_years_inspection_handbook.pdf (accessed 25 May 2015)

Ofsted, Notifications: http://www.ofsted.gov.uk/sites/default/files/documents/other-forms-and-guides/n/Notification%20of%20serious%20childcare%20incident.pdf (accessed 6 May 2015)

O'Neill, D. http://www.getsurrey.co.uk/news/nursery-fined-after-two-year-old-boy-6520361 (accessed 6 May 2015)

Orola, S. case: http://www.dailymail.co.uk/news/article-2152186/Five-year-old-boy-attempting-forward-roll-nursery-school-climbing-frame-fell-died-heart-attack.html (accessed 6 May 2015)

Pitcher, J. case: http://news.bbc.co.uk/1/hi/england/london/8399514.stm (accessed 6 May 2015)

Public Health England guidance, 'Guidance on infection control in schools and other child care settings': https://www.gov.uk/government/uploads/system/uploads/attachment_data/file/353953/Guidance_on_infection_control_in_schools_11_Sept.pdf (accessed 22 May 2015)

Public Health England report, 'Reducing unintentional injuries in and around the home among children under five years'. 2014. PHE publications

Public Health England: https://www.gov.uk/government/news/drowning-in-baths-a-risk-for-young-children-warns-phe (accessed 6 May 2015)

Punchline: http://www.punchline-gloucester.com/articles/december2014/cheltenhamchildrensnurseryprosecutedafterasbestosexposure#sthash.RyHsk8u8.dpuf (accessed 6 May 2015)

Rae, A. case: http://news.bbc.co.uk/go/pr/fr/-/1/hi/england/coventry_warwickshire/4837614.stm (accessed 6 May 2015)

Recalls: http://search.which.co.uk/search?w=product+recalls&asug=&mainresult=mainresult%3Ayes (accessed 6 May

Reporting of Injuries, Diseases and Dangerous Occurrences Regulations 2013 (RIDDOR) http://www.legislation.gov.uk/uksi/2013/1471/contents/made (accessed 23/10/15)

RIDDOR Consultation: Source: CD 243, 'Public consultation on proposals to simplify and clarify RIDDOR reporting requirements' http://www.hse.gov.uk/consult/condocs/cd243.htm

RoSPA campaign regarding electric gates: http://www.rospa.com/campaigns-fundraising/current/electric-gates/ (accessed 6 May 2015)

RoSPA: http://www.rospa.com/homesafety/currentcampaigns/nappysacks/ (accessed 6 May 2015)

RoSPA: http://www.rospa.com/homesafety/adviceandinformation/product/button-cell-batteries.aspx (accessed 6 May 2015)

RoSPA Position Statements, September 2014: http://www.rospa.com/rospaweb/docs/advice-services/home-safety/rospa-home-safety-position-statements.pdf (accessed 6 May 2015)

RoSPA: http://www.rospa.com/home-safety/advice/general/facts-and-figures/ (accessed 6 May 2015)

RoSPA: http://www.rospa.com/home-safety/advice/child-safety/accidents-to-children/ (accessed 6 May 2015)

RoSPA: http://www.rospa.com/leisure-safety/statistics/drowning/ (accessed 6 May 2015)

Safety Assured Limited: http://www.fingerprotector.co.uk (accessed 6 May 2015)

Salmonella case: http://www.thecourier.co.uk/news/health/salmonella-bug-hits-west-fife-nursery-toddlers-1.26333 (accessed 6 May 2015)

Salmonella case: http://www.eveningtelegraph.co.uk/news/local/dundee-nursery-kids-get-salmonella-bug-1.140742 (accessed 6 May 2015)

Section 3(1) of the Health and Safety at Work Etc. Act 1974

Evening Standard: http://www.standard.co.uk/news/nursery-admits-guilt-over-baby-death-6986169.html (accessed 6 May 2015)

St John Ambulance: http://www.sja.org.uk/sja/support-us/our-campaigns/baby-choking-the-chokeables.aspx?utm_source=NHQ&utm_medium=Short+URL&utm_term=the-chokeables&utm_content=textlink&utm_campaign=the+chokeables (accessed 6 May 2015)

Stockham, K. case: http://news.bbc.co.uk/1/hi/england/bristol/5260538.stm (accessed 6 May 2015)

TB case: http://news.bbc.co.uk/1/hi/scotland/2691753.stm (accessed 6 May 2015)

TB case: http://news.bbc.co.uk/1/hi/wales/north_East/7925639.stm (accessed 6 May 2015)

TB case: http://www.heraldscotland.com/news/health/children-to-be-screened-as-nursery-worker-catches-tb.15224861 (accessed 6 May 2015)

TB case: http://www.mirror.co.uk/news/uk-news/nursery-hit-by-tb-scare-348021 (accessed 6 May 2015)

TB case: http://www.scotsman.com/news/health/motherwell-nursery-worker-tests-positive-for-tb-1-3394562 (accessed 6 May 2015)

TB case: http://www.telegraph.co.uk/news/uknews/1329888/Three-children-at-nursery-have-TB.html (accessed 6 May 2015)

TB case: http://m.theargus.co.uk/news/12952116.Parents_in_uproar_about_delay_in_warning_of_TB_infected_person_at_nursery/?ref=mac (accessed 6 May 2015)

Two-year-old boy: http://www.getsurrey.co.uk/news/nursery-fined-after-two-year-old-boy-6520361 (accessed 6 May 2015)

Visit My Farm: http://www.visitmyfarm.org/component/k2/item/339-industry-code-of-practice (accessed 6 May 2015)

White, C. case: http://news.bbc.co.uk/1/hi/england/7747854.stm (accessed 6 May 2015)

Williams, K. case: http://www.dailymail.co.uk/news/article-1020519/Headmaster-blamed-death-pupil-playground-fall-wins-appeal-conviction.html (accessed 6 May 2015)

Wiseman, J. case: http://www.dailymail.co.uk/news/article-371191/Toddler-choked-death-meatball.html#ixzz27VknniTL (accessed 6 May 2015)

World Health Organsiation (WHO): http://www.who.int/campaigns/world-health-day/2015/ fact-sheet.pdf (accessed 6 May 2015)

World Health Organisation (WHO): http://www.who.int/topics/foodborne_diseases/en/ (accessed 31 May 2015)

World Health Organisation (WHO): http://www.who.int/topics/infectious_diseases/en/ (accessed 31 May 2015)

Work at Height regulations 2005:) http://www.legislation.gov.uk/uksi/2005/735/regulation/12/ made (accessed 23/10/15)

Useful links

Allergies and asthma

Allergies: http://www.allergyuk.org (accessed 6 May 2015)
Anaphylaxis: http://www.anaphylaxis.org.uk (accessed 6 May 2015)
Asthma: http://www.asthma.org.uk/advice-nursery-and-childcare (accessed 29 May 2015)
Coeliac: https://www.coeliac.org.uk/home/ (accessed 6 May 2015)
New Allergen information rules: https://www.food.gov.uk/news-updates/campaigns/
    allergen-rules

Burns and scalds

Children's Burns Trust (CBT): http://www.cbtrust.org.uk/ (accessed 6 May 2015)
Child Safety Europe: http://www.childsafetyeurope.org/injurytopics/burnsandscalds/
    (accessed 6 May 2015)

Buildings

Asbestos: http://www.beware-asbestos.info (accessed 6 May 2015)
HSE: http://www.hse.gov.uk/asbestos/ (accessed 6 May 2015)
HSE: Asbestos Health and Safety Executive. Publication: http://www.hse.gov.uk/pubns/
    indg223.pdf (accessed 6 May 2015)

Child Action Prevention Trust (CAPT)

http://www.capt.org.uk/who-we-are/news/bbc-highlights-dangers-button-batteries-one-
    show (accessed 6 May 2015)
http://www.capt.org.uk/resources/talking-about-strangulation pdf (accessed 6 May 2015)
CAPT ongoing safety campaigns: http://www.capt.org.uk/?gclid=CMeDj6aSrcUCFSLlwgod_
    AwA2w (accessed 6 May 2015)
http://capt.org.uk/what-we-do/training-consultancy-mentoring/consultancy-services/
    targeted-awareness-campaigns (accessed 6 May 2015)
http://www.capt.org.uk/safety-advice/keeping-your-child-safe-drowning) (accessed 6 May
    2015)
http://www.capt.org.uk/resources/drowning (accessed 6 May 2015)
http://www.capt.org.uk/safety-advice/protecting-your-child-burns-and-scalds (accessed 6 May
    2015)

Coroners' Reports

https://www.gov.uk/government/uploads/system/uploads/attachment_data/file/217348/
summary-rule-43–070312.pdf (accessed 6 May 2015)

Deaths in day care settings

Bishop, L. case: http://www.nurseryworld.co.uk/nursery-world/news/1141957/york-college-
nursery-lydia-bishops-death-completely-avoidable (accessed 6 May 2015) Coulson, J: 'R v
York College, Leeds Crown Court 14 February 2014 Sentencing Remarks of Coulson J' https://
www.judiciary.gov.uk/wp-content/uploads/JCO/Documents/Judgments/r-v-york-college.pdf
(accessed 24 October 2015)

Chauhan, T. case: http://www.dailymail.co.uk/news/article-2202297/Dicky-Birds-nursery-Police-
investigate-death-year-old-Tiya-Chauhan-choked-jelly-cube.html (accessed 6 May 2015)

Cunliffe, M. case: http://news.bbc.co.uk/1/hi/england/gloucestershire/6273602.stm (accessed
6 May 2015) http://www.dailymail.co.uk/news/article-1081542/Nursery-owner-ordered-
pay-55–000-showing-gross-incompetence-toddler-strangled-clothes-bag.html (accessed
24 October 2015)

Egan, T. case: http://news.bbc.co.uk/1/hi/england/2702111.stm (accessed 6 May 2015)

Hollick, G. case: http://www.telegraph.co.uk/news/uknews/4969646/Nursery-company-fined-
145000-for-baby-choking-death.html (accessed 6 May 2015)

Ladwa, O. case: http://www.dailymail.co.uk/news/article-450954/Toddler-crushed-death-
ambulance-thought-warnings-game.html (accessed 6 May 2015)

Lindsay, C. case: http://news.bbc.co.uk/1/hi/england/hereford/worcs/4887892.stm (accessed
6 May 2015) http://www.telegraph.co.uk/news/uknews/1515123/Parents-will-be-haunted-
forever-by-face-of-baby-who-died-at-nursery.html (accessed 24 october 2015)

Malin, R. case:
http://www.dailymail.co.uk/news/article-2350782/Nursery-nurse-fined-just-2–400-toddler-
care-hanged--promoted-THREE-TIMES-tragedy.html (accessed 24 October 2015)

Milner, A. case: http://www.dailymail.co.uk/news/article-1232942/Toddler-dies-choking-
sausage-nursery.html#ixzz27Pcs8Xu6 (accessed 6 May 2015)

Orola, S. case: http://www.dailymail.co.uk/news/article-2152186/Five-year-old-boy-
attempting-forward-roll-nursery-school-climbing-frame-fell-died-heart-attack.html
(accessed 6 May 2015)

Rae, A. case: http://news.bbc.co.uk/go/pr/fr/-/1/hi/england/coventry_warwickshire/
4837614.stm (accessed 6 May 2015)

Stockham, K. case: http://news.bbc.co.uk/1/hi/england/bristol/5260538.stm (accessed 6 May
2015)

Thompson, M. case: http://www.bbc.co.uk/news/uk-england-manchester-25232661 (accessed
6 May 2015)

Williams, K. case: http://www.dailymail.co.uk/news/article-1020519/Headmaster-blamed-
death-pupil-playground-fall-wins-appeal-conviction.html (accessed 6 May 2015)

Wiseman, J. case: http://www.dailymail.co.uk/news/article-371191/Toddler-choked-death-meatball.html#ixzz27VknniTL (accessed 6 May 2015)

EYFS

Early years outcomes: https://www.gov.uk/government/publications/early-years-outcomes (accessed 6 May 2015)

Department for Education, Statutory framework for the early years foundation stage, 2014: https://www.gov.uk/government/uploads/system/uploads/attachment_data/file/335504/EYFS_framework_from_1_September_2014__with_clarification_note.pdf (accessed 6 May 2015)

Falls

http://www.childsafetyeurope.org/injurytopics/falls/ (accessed 6 May 2015)

The European Child Safety Alliance, Childhood Falls. 2009 http://www.childsafetyeurope.org/injurytopics/falls/ (accessed 21 October 2015)

http://www.rospa.com/rospaweb/docs/advice-services/home-safety/rospa-home-safety-position-statements.pdf (accessed 6 May 2015)

E. coli cases

http://www.dailymail.co.uk/health/article-149458/Nursery-youngsters-battle-E-coli-bug.html (accessed 26 May 2015)

http://www.nurseryworld.co.uk/nursery-world/news/1081752/study-puffins-pre-school-brecon-wales (accessed 26 May 2015)

http://www.theguardian.com/uk/2006/may/14/health.healthandwellbeing (accessed 26 May 2015)

http://www.manchestereveningnews.co.uk/news/greater-manchester-news/ecoli-probe-at-nursery-930229 (accessed 26 May 2015)

http://www.eastbourneherald.co.uk/news/local/e-coli-outbreak-closes-hellingly-nursery-1–1435379 (accessed 26 May 2015)

http://www.wales.nhs.uk/sitesplus/862/news/20701 (accessed 26 May 2015)

http://www.walesonline.co.uk/news/local-news/nursery-playgroup-re-open-after-bangor-1797949 (accessed 26 May 2015)

http://news.stv.tv/north/193121-child-left-blind-and-deaf-following-ecoli-outbreak-at-nursery/ (accessed 26 May 2015)

http://www.bournemouthecho.co.uk/news/11625959.UPDATE__Council_nursery_closes_its_doors_after_E_coll_outbreak_hospitalises_pre_school_children/?ref=mr (accessed 26 May 2015)

http://www.bbc.co.uk/news/uk-england-merseyside-28152470 (accessed 26 May 2015)
http://www.lancashiretelegraph.co.uk/news/11562242.Two_children_in_hospital_
    following_E_coll_outbreak_at_East_Lancs_nursery/?ref=rss (accessed 26 May 2015)
http://www.bbc.co.uk/news/uk-england-tees-32732974 (accessed 26 May 2015)

First aid

Millie's Campaign: https://www.gov.uk/government/news/first-aid-training-to-be-made-
    compulsory-for-new-nursery-recruits (accessed 6 May 2015)
St John Ambulance: http://www.sja.org.uk/sja/support-us/our-campaigns/baby-choking-
    the-chokeables.aspx?utm_source=NHQ&utm_medium=Short+URL&utm_term=the-
    chokeables&utm_content=textlink&utm_campaign=the+chokeables (accessed 6 May 2015)

Finger protectors

Children's Charter Door Safety Standard: http://www.childrens-charter.org/doorsafetystandard.html
    (accessed 31 May 2015)

Food

Campylobacter guide: http://www.food.gov.uk/news-updates/campaigns/campylobacter/
    fsw-2014
E. coli guide: https://www.food.gov.uk/business-industry/guidancenotes/hygguid/ecoliguide
EC Regulation No. 852/2004 On the hygiene of foodstuffs: http://eur-lex.europa.eu/legal-
    content/EN/TXT/?uri=uriserv:OJ.L_.2004.226.01.0003.01.ENG (accessed 31 May 2015)
EU Food Information for Consumers Regulation (No. 1169/2011): http://eur-lex.europa.eu/
    legal-content/EN/TXT/?uri=CELEX:32011R1169 (accessed 31 May 2015)
Food Safety Act 1990 (as amended): http://www.legislation.gov.uk/ukpga/1990/16/contents
    (accessed 31 May 2015)
Food Standards Agency (FSA): http://allergytraining.food.gov.uk/english/food-allergy-facts.
    aspx (accessed 6 May 2015)
https://www.food.gov.uk/sites/default/files/multimedia/pdfs/publication/loosefoodsleaflet.
    pdf (accessed 6 May 2015)
https://www.food.gov.uk/sites/default/files/multimedia/pdfs/publication/allergy-labelling-
    prepacked.pdf (accessed 6 May 2015)
https://www.food.gov.uk/sites/default/files/multimedia/pdfs/publication/
    allergencontrollaeho1208.pdf (accessed 6 May 2015)
https://www.food.gov.uk/enforcement/enforcetrainfund/onlinetraining/allergytraining
    (accessed 6 May 2015)
https://www.food.gov.uk/news-updates/news/allergy-alerts-news (accessed 6 May 2015)

Health and Safety Executive (HSE)

Asbestos: http://www.hse.gov.uk/asbestos/ (accessed 6 May 2015)

E. coli: http://www.hse.gov.uk/campaigns/farmsafe/ecoli.htm (accessed 6 May 2015)

First aid: http://www.hse.gov.uk/firstaid/ (accessed 6 May 2015)First aid: http://www.hse.gov.uk/pubns/books/l174.htm (accessed 23 May 2015)

Inquests: http://www.hse.gov.uk/enforce/enforcementguide/wrdeaths/chronology.htm (accessed 6 May 2015)

Investigating accidents: http://www.hse.gov.uk/managing/delivering/check/investigating-accidents-incidents.htm (accessed 6 May 2015)

Managing: http://www.hse.gov.uk/managing/plan-do-check-act.htm (accessed 23 May 2015)

Myth: http://www.hse.gov.uk/myth/september.htm (accessed 6 May 2015)

RIDDOR: http://www.hse.gov.uk/riddor (accessed 31 May 2015)

RIDDOR Reporting: http://www.hse.gov.uk/riddor/report.htm (accessed 31 May 2015)

Risk: http://www.hse.gov.uk/Risk/ (accessed 6 May 2015)

Publication: http://www.hse.gov.uk/pubns/books/hsg65.htm (accessed 25 May 2015)

Publication: http://www.hse.gov.uk/pubns/indg223.pdf (accessed 6 May 2015)

Salford prosecution: http://press.hse.gov.uk/2014/salford-council-prosecuted-after-child-loses-fingertips-in-school-gate/?ebul=hsegen&cr=10/14-apr-14 (accessed 6 May 2015)

School trips: http://www.hse.gov.uk/services/education/school-trips.htm (accessed 6 May 2015)

Training: http://www.hse.gov.uk/pubns/indg345.pdf (accessed 6 May 2015)

Health and Safety at Work Etc. Act 1974

Health and Safety (First Aid) Regulations 1981 http://www.legislation.gov.uk/uksi/1981/917/contents/made (accessed 23/10/15)

Hull City Council: http://www.hullcc.gov.uk?portal/page?_pageid=221,674011&_dad=potal&_scheme (accessed 6 May 2015)

Independent: http://www.independent.co.uk/news/uk/this-britain/nursery-is-fined-60000-over-death-of-allergic-baby-93930.html (accessed 6 May 2015)

Infection control: https://www.gov.uk/government/uploads/system/uploads/attachment_data/file/353953/Guidance_on_infection_control_in_schools_11_Sept.pdf (accessed 6 May 2015)

Inspection

Common inspection framework: education, skills and early years from September 2015: https://www.gov.uk/government/publications/common-inspection-framework-education-skills-and-early-years-from-september-2015 (accessed 6 August 2015)

Fundamental British Values: http://www.foundationyears.org.uk/files/2015/03/Fundamental_British_Values.pdf (accessed 6 August 2015)

EYPP: https://www.gov.uk/early-years-pupil-premium-guide-for-local-authorities (accessed 6 August 2015)

Ofsted examples of good practice: https://www.gov.uk/government/collections/ofsted-examples-of-good-practice-in-early-years (accessed 6 August 2015)

Injuries to children in day care settings

'A child' case: http://www.swindonadvertiser.co.uk/news/11104567.display/ (accessed 27 May 2015)

Ahmed, E. case: http://www.telegraph.co.uk/education/educationnews/9562575/Nursery-fined-over-cover-up-after-fall-left-child-in-a-coma.html (accessed 6 May 2015)

Brooker, F. case: http://www.dailymail.co.uk/news/article-2602344/Parents-threatened-having-15-month-old-daughter-taken-away-social-services-suffers-unexplainable-burns-blisters-fingers-NURSERY.html (accessed 6 May 2015)

Busby. L. case:

http://www.hullcc.gov.uk/portal/page?_pageid=221,674011&_dad=portal&_schema=PORTAL&p_id=4847

(accessed 24 Octoberay 2015)

Bush, M. case: http://www.southwalesargus.co.uk/news/9867659.Newport_girl_was_injured_with_pair_of_scissors_at_nursery/

Cannock House Day Nursery:

http://www.newsshopper.co.uk/news/4402651.CHELSFIELD_____40_000_fine_after_nursery_salmonella_outbreak

(accessed 24 October 2015)

Coniff, B. case: http://www.birminghammail.co.uk/news/local-news/shard-end-nursery-closure-call-6181881 (accessed 27 May 2015)

Dedek, S. case: http://www.dailymail.co.uk/news/article-2272991/Sophie-Dedek-Our-daughters-finger-severed-nursery-door-staff-realised-floor.html

Dosanjh, D. case: http://www.coventrytelegraph.net/news/coventry-news/coventry-school-staffs-fight-save-3035168

Dunseath, B. case: http://www.bbc.co.uk/news/uk-northern-ireland-21011892 (accessed 6 May 2015)

Eaton, M. case: http://www.birminghammail.co.uk/news/local-news/three-year-old-girl-nearly-blinded-fall-6448345 (accessed 27 May 2015)

Frith, C. case: http://www.dailymail.co.uk/news/article-2124043/Chantelle-Firth-Pentland-Primary-School-student-6-dies-choking-lunch.html (accessed 6 May 2015)

Gregson, K. case: http://www.nottinghampost.com/Child-s-finger-severed-school-door/story-12239522-detail/story.html (accessed 6 May 2015)

Holt, S. case: http://vscg.co.uk/case-law/stamford_park_hse_prosecution (accessed 6 May 2015)

Farrel, H. case: http://www.dailymail.co.uk/news/article-2358766/Mother-sues-nursery-staff-spilt-burning-CHICKEN-FAT-year-old-son-leaving-second-degree-burns.html (accessed 6 May 2015)

Lumsden, K. case: http://www.dailymail.co.uk/news/article-2376182/Toddlers-thumb-ripped-nursery-trapped-door-wall.html (accessed 6 May 2015)

McGinty, R. case: http://www.dailyrecord.co.uk/news/local-news/furious-couple-slam-nursery-after-4446471 (accessed 27 May 2015)

Miller, M. case: http://www.personalinjuryclaimsbradford.co.uk/Blog/personal-injury-claims/5-year-old-receives-compensation-for-nursery-injury.html (accessed 6 May 2015)

Nine-year-old boy: http://press.hse.gov.uk/2014/bolton-charity-in-court-after-child-loses-finger-in-school-door/ (accessed 6 May 2015)

Pearce, I. case: http://www.dailymail.co.uk/news/article-2970633/Girl-13-suffered-rare-form-autism-choked-death-meatball-school-canteen.html (accessed 6 May 2015)

Pitcher, J. case: http://news.bbc.co.uk/1/hi/england/london/8399514.stm (accessed 6 May 2015)

Six-year-old boy: http://press.hse.gov.uk/2014/salford-council-prosecuted-after-child-loses-fingertips-in-school-gate/?ebul=hsegen&cr=10/14-apr-14 (accessed 6 May 2015)

Two-year-old boy: http://www.getsurrey.co.uk/news/nursery-fined-after-two-year-old-boy-6520361

Hunt, M. case: http://www.birminghammail.co.uk/news/local-news/nursery-guilt-over-tots-scalding-41331 (accessed 6 May 2015)

White, C. case: http://news.bbc.co.uk/1/hi/england/7747854.stm

NHS

http://www.patientsafetyfirst.nhs.uk/ashx/Asset.ashx?path=/Intervention-support/FALLSHow-to%20Guide%20v4.pdf (accessed 6 May 2015)

http://www.nhs.uk/Conditions/Burns-and-scalds/Pages/Introduction.aspx (accessed 6 May 2015)

Notifiable diseases

Government website: https://www.gov.uk/notifiable-diseases-and-causative-organisms-how-to-report (accessed 31 May 2015)

Nursery World magazine

Gaunt, C. 14 January 2013. http://www.nurseryworld.co.uk/nursery-world/news/1097515/exclusive-concern-lack-nursery-deaths-injuries (accessed 6 May 2015)

Ofsted

Early Years compliance handbook (Updated September 2015): https://www.gov.uk/government/publications/compliance-investigation-and-enforcement-handbook-childcare (accessed 21 October 2015)

: https://www.gov.uk/government/publications/compliance-investigation-and-enforcement-handbook-childcare (accessed 6 May 2015)

Early years inspection handbook from September 2015 https://www.gov.uk/government/publications/early-years-inspection-handbook-from-september-2015 (accessed 21 October 2015)

Notifications: http://www.ofsted.gov.uk/sites/default/files/documents/other-forms-and-guides/n/Notification%20of%20serious%20childcare%20incident.pdf (accessed 6 May 2015)

Public Health England

Public Health England Guidance, 'Guidance on infection control in schools and other child care settings': https://www.gov.uk/government/uploads/system/uploads/attachment_data/file/353953/Guidance_on_infection_control_in_schools_11_Sept.pdf (accessed 22 May 2015)

Public Health England report, 'Reducing unintentional injuries in and around the home among children under five years'. 2014. PHE publications

Public Health England: https://www.gov.uk/government/news/drowning-in-baths-a-risk-for-young-children-warns-phe (accessed 6 May 2015)

RoSPA

ROSPA campaign regarding electric gates: http://www.rospa.com/campaigns-fundraising/current/electric-gates/ (accessed 6 May 2015)

http://www.rospa.com/homesafety/currentcampaigns/nappysacks/ (accessed 6 May 2015)

http://www.rospa.com/homesafety/adviceandinformation/product/button-cell-batteries.aspx (accessed 6 May 2015)

RoSPA Position Statements, September 2014: http://www.rospa.com/rospaweb/docs/advice-services/home-safety/rospa-home-safety-position-statements.pdf (accessed 21 October 2015)

http://www.rospa.com/home-safety/advice/general/facts-and-figures/ (accessed 6 May 2015)

http://www.rospa.com/home-safety/advice/child-safety/accidents-to-children/ (accessed 6 May 2015)

http://www.rospa.com/leisure-safety/statistics/drowning/ (accessed 6 May 2015)

Salmonella cases

http://www.thecourier.co.uk/news/health/salmonella-bug-hits-west-fife-nursery-toddlers-1.26333 (accessed 26 May 2015)

http://www.eveningtelegraph.co.uk/news/local/dundee-nursery-kids-get-salmonella-bug-1.140742 (accessed 26 May 2015)

http://www.newsshopper.co.uk/news/4402651.CHELSFIELD_____40_000_fine_after_nursery_salmonella_outbreak (accessed 24 October 2015)

Safety campaigns

Button batteries: Newcastle: http://www.newcastle.gov.uk/business/trading-standards/
campaigns/safety-of-button-cell-batteries (accessed 6 May 2015)

Childalert: http://www.childalert.co.uk/safety.php?tab=Safety (accessed 6 May 2015)

Children's Charter: http://www.childrens-charter.org/index.html) (accessed 6 May 2015)

Drowning: http://drowningpreventionweek.org.uk/ (accessed 6 May 2015)

'Make it safe': http://www.makeitsafe.org.uk (accessed 6 May 2015)

Recalls: http://search.which.co.uk/search?w=product+recalls&asug=&mainresult=mainresult%
3Ayes (accessed 6 May 2015)

World Health Organisation: http://www.who.int/campaigns/world-health-day/2015/fact-
sheet.pdf (accessed 6 May 2015)

TB cases

http://www.telegraph.co.uk/news/uknews/1329888/Three-children-at-nursery-have-TB.html
(accessed 29 May 2015)

http://news.bbc.co.uk/1/hi/scotland/2691753.stm (accessed 29 May 2015)

http://news.bbc.co.uk/1/hi/scotland/2691753.stm (accessed 29 May 2015)

http://www.mirror.co.uk/news/uk-news/nursery-hit-by-tb-scare-348021 (accessed 29 May
2015)

http://news.bbc.co.uk/1/hi/wales/north_East/7925639.stm (accessed 29 May 2015)

http://www.heraldscotland.com/news/health/children-to-be-screened-as-nursery-worker-
catches-tb.15224861 (accessed 29 May 2015)

http://www.scotsman.com/news/health/motherwell-nursery-worker-tests-positive-for-tb-
1–3394562 (accessed 29 May 2015)

http://m.theargus.co.uk/news/12952116.Parents_in_uproar_about_delay_in_warning_of_TB_
infected_person_at_nursery/?ref=mac (accessed 29 May 2015)

Index